U.S. Fish & Wildlife Service

Shared Commitments to Conservation

*2000 Annual Report of the
U.S. Fish & Wildlife Service*

ERRATA SHEET
FISCAL YEAR 2000 ANNUAL REPORT
U.S. FISH & WILDLIFE SERVICE

Subsequent to printing of the U.S. Fish & Wildlife Fiscal Year 2000 Annual Report, the following errors were detected. Errors and their corrections are cited below.

Page 37, Subtitle, *Analysis of Revenues and Financing Sources,* first sentence, as printed, reads, "In FY 2000, the Service's total financing sources amounted to $2.282 billion, which is...."

This sentence should read, "In FY 2000, the Service's total financing sources amounted to $2.263 billion, which is...."

Page 40, CONSOLIDATED STATEMENT OF FINANCIAL POSITION, Construction in Progress (Note 6), amount as printed, reads, "$2,829"

This amount should read, "$82,829"

Page 42, Heading, CONSOLIDATED STATEMENT OF NET COST FOR THE YEAR ENDED SEPTEMBER 30, 2000

"(DOLLARS IN THOUSANDS)" should be included as the final line of this heading

Pages 50, Note 9. *Unexpended Appropriations.* As printed, this Note and its text should be placed in front of the table, titled *Unexpended Appropriations as of September 30, 2000,* found on Page 49 of the report at the bottom of the third column.

Page 80, Heading, Supplemental Information, *Performance Costs under the Service's Program Goals.*

"(Dollars in Thousands)" should be included as the final line of this heading

The United States Fish and Wildlife Service
History and Mission

As an asset of tremendous environmental, recreational, and economic importance, this nation's fish and wildlife resources represent a vital part of our natural heritage — one that is facing increasing pressures every day. For this reason, the mission of the U.S. Fish and Wildlife Service (Service) grows more complex and critical every day. As the Service continues to look for new and better ways to conserve, protect, and enhance fish and wildlife and their habitat, its major responsibilities remain focused on migratory birds, endangered species, certain marine mammals, and freshwater and anadromous fish.

History of the Service
The Service's origins date back to 1871 when Congress established the U.S. Fish Commission to study the decrease in the nation's food fish and recommend ways to reverse the decline. Placed under the Department of Commerce in 1903, it was renamed the Bureau of Fisheries. Meanwhile Congress created an Office of Economic Ornithology in the Department of Agriculture in 1885 to study the food habits and migratory patterns of birds, especially those that had an effect on agriculture. After several more name changes, this office was renamed the Bureau of Biological Survey in 1905.

The Bureaus of Fisheries and Biological Survey were transferred to the Department of the Interior in 1939 and in 1940 were combined and named the Fish and Wildlife Service. Further reorganization came in 1956 when the Fish and Wildlife Act created the United States Fish and Wildlife Service and established within the agency two separate bureaus — Commercial Fisheries and Sport Fisheries and Wildlife.

The Bureau of Commercial Fisheries was transferred to the Department of Commerce in 1970 and is now known as the National Marine Fisheries Service. The Bureau of Sport Fisheries and Wildlife remained in Interior. In 1974, the "Bureau" name was dropped and the agency is now simply called the U.S. Fish and Wildlife Service. In 1993, the Service's research activities were transferred to the U.S. Geological Survey.

Today, Service employees number approximately 7,500 individuals located close to fish and wildlife resources throughout the country. Offices and facilities are located in Washington, D.C., seven regional offices, and in nearly 700 field units, including 70 national fish hatcheries and over 500 national wildlife refuges.

Mission of the Service
The Service's mission is, working with others, to conserve, protect and enhance fish, wildlife and plants and their habitats for the continuing benefit of the American people.

Since before recorded history, fish and wildlife resources in the United States have been an integral part of human life. We know that the earliest Americans depended on fish and wildlife for both life sustenance and spiritual nourishment. The kinship of aboriginal Americans to these resources is seen today in their religious and cultural activities. The sea turtle is viewed as the symbol of eternal life with the great creator. Salmon and other anadromous fishes were and still are celebrated as symbols of the renewal of life. Wildlife served as the spiritual connection with ones ancestors and the creator of all life.

When settlers came to America, they found a land teeming with wildlife. Like Native Americans, they depended on the land's rich wildlife heritage for food and clothing. Colonies were located near rivers for commerce and travel and for a rich supply of fish and wildlife for food. The new settlers fully intended that freedom to hunt for food and to secure water for life would be the right of all, regardless of heritage or status. The framers of our Constitution recognized this and placed great emphasis on natural rights and natural laws. Because of the American ideal to respect fish and wildlife as a resource available for the use and enjoyment of all, it is revered as a public trust resource — a resource deserving the public's attention and participatory guidance. The United States continues to refine the body of case law and statutes governing the stewardship of fish and wildlife resources.

Communities and people throughout the United States have a strong commitment to the fish and wildlife resources today. Many communities realize tremendous economic benefits from tourism and visitors that come specifically to enjoy watching and pursuing fish and wildlife. Hunting and fishing remain strong components of community culture all along the great river systems of the nation. Americans value and respect their natural resource heritage.

The U.S. Fish and Wildlife Service has the privilege of being the primary agency responsible for the protection, conservation, and renewal of these resources for this and future generations. We accept this responsibility and challenge with optimism and resolve to pass along to future generations of stewards a fish and wildlife resource heritage that is as strong or stronger than when it was entrusted to us.

Message from the Acting Director and the Chief Financial Officer

The year 2000 marks the turn of the millenium, an event of a lifetime that only a few generations will experience. We are fortunate to be of this time and at the U.S. Fish and Wildlife Service, it is true in more ways than one. Through our cooperative efforts with our public and partners, we are maximizing our effectiveness on the ground. Together we are magnifying our conservation efforts and reaping the benefits of our shared commitments to conservation.

The Service, by applying the ecosystem approach to natural resource management, is putting into practice ecosystem principles such as cross program collaboration within the Service and partnership building outside the Service. Ecosystem strategies are designed to meet the collective needs of natural resource regions in the aggregate. Our collective strength lies in the diversity of our partners and in the effectiveness of our programs. Our joint effectiveness lies in our ability to find common benefits by dovetailing priorities and challenges on the landscape level. We are building a future for shared commitments to conservation through building lasting partnerships today.

This Annual Report is testimony to our partnerships that have enhanced fish and wildlife resources through innovative and cooperative management. It provides a road map of the Service's future direction, an overview of the Service's diverse programs and accomplishments, and an accounting for the funds used by the Service. The Stewardship and Program Highlights sections provide detailed information on the role of the Service in maintaining healthy environments that fish and wildlife need throughout the nation and the world. Under Supplemental Information, the Service provides information on the costs of attaining performance under each of the Service's mission goals established for Fffi 2000.

We hope that this report helps you better understand what we do, how much fish and wildlife and plants depend on our shared commitments to conservation, the costs of our efforts, and how much more we can accomplish by working together.

Marshall P. Jones, Jr.
Acting Director,
U.S. Fish & Wildlife Service

Table of Contents

Program Highlights
Shared Commitments to Conservation

Meeting the challenges of providing and protecting a healthy environment for fish and wildlife and for people is central to the programs of the U.S. Fish and Wildlife Service (Service) and is firmly based on tradition since its predecessor agencies were established more than a century ago. Meeting these challenges requires the cooperation and support of other Federal agencies, State and local governments, foreign governments, conservation groups, and local communities. Dedicated Americans, combined with our dedicated International partners, are sharing a common commitment to conservation and are working hand-in-hand with the Service to ensure that our Nation's irreplaceable natural heritage and the world's fish and wildlife resources are protected for the enjoyment of this and future generations.

Portions of this narrative reference specific program accomplishments achieved under the Service's mission or strategic goals identified in its revised 5-Year Strategic Plan. This year the Service selected a subset of specific strategic goals, one for each of the three mission goals, under which to report specific program performance in this report. Another, more comprehensive report on all program achievements under each strategic and mission goal presented in the Service's 5-Year Strategic Plan can be found in the Service's budget documents. The purpose of this report is to highlight general program achievements of the Service, in cooperation with its partners, in a structure that parallels its three mission goals which are: (1) sustaining fish and wildlife populations; (2) conserving habitat; and, (3) linking wildlife and people through fostering public use and enjoyment of fish and wildlife resources. Further, the Service completed its Statement of Net Cost, whereby the Service identifies its expenditures to meet each of the three mission goals. Please refer to both sections, the Message from the Chief Financial Officer and the Financial Statements, for detailed information on how the Service identified these costs and allocated them to each mission goal.

Sustaining Fish and Wildlife Populations
Many of the nation's and the world's native fish, wildlife and plant populations are declining or are at historic low levels due to habitat degradation, inadequate fish passage, over-use, poaching, illegal trade in wildlife and wildlife products, introductions of invasive or nonindigenous species, poor land management practices, or urbanization. In partnership with other Federal, State and tribal governments, foreign governments, and a variety of private interests, the Service is effectively contributing to the conservation of fish, wildlife and plants, both nationally and worldwide.

The Service emphasizes proactive species conservation for many species of fish, wildlife, and plants through the Candidate Conservation Program. Candidate species are species for which the Service has sufficient biological information to indicate that listing is warranted. The goal of our Candidate Conservation Program is to prevent listing of species under the Endangered Species Act (ESA). This program takes a collaborative approach with States and Territories, other Federal agencies and the private sector to identify species that need conservation and then cooperatively conserve those species. Early action is important because simpler, more cost-effective conservation options are made available and conservation is more likely to be ultimately successful. Also, potential conflicts caused by species listing may be avoided and flexibility for landowners and land managers can be maintained.

Through Candidate Conservation Agreements (CCAs), the Service works with its partners to identify threats to candidate species, plan measures needed to stabilize and conserve them, identify willing landowners, develop and implement conservation measures, and monitor their effectiveness. Candidate Conservation Agreements with Assurances assure non-federal landowners that they can continue agreed-upon activities even if the species becomes listed in the future. Landowners are

The Service entered into a new national partnership with the Center for Plant Conservation that will enhance the recovery of listed plants.

increasingly working with the Service to undertake conservation efforts for candidate species, and in return, are receiving regulatory assurances. The Service uses both CCAs and Candidate Conservation Agreements with Assurances to work with partners to conserve species. In some cases, such as the Pecos pupfish and Goodings onion, conservation has precluded the need to list. During FY 2000, the Service implemented more than five conservation agreements covering six species, for which the Service hopes to prevent listing. Monitoring of CCAs ensures that biological goals for the covered species are achieved and that threats to the species are reduced. As the success for this program grows, so does the demand for new agreements.

Even with these successes, there is much work to be done. As of August 16, 2000, 246 plant and animal species were candidates for listing under the ESA, more than 100 of which are highly threatened with extinction. Another 37 species proposed for listing can benefit from candidate conservation actions. As

of August 3, 2000, the Service had 14 active lawsuits covering more than 23 species regarding petition findings, 7 active lawsuits covering more than 9 species regarding final determinations, 33 active lawsuits covering more than 329 species regarding critical habitat, and 4 active lawsuits covering more than 4 species regarding merit challenges. In addition, the Service received 67 Notices of Intent (NOIs) to sue (involving more than 193 species) relative to listing activities. The Service developed a prioritized list of listing actions for each region that specifies how the FY 2000 appropriation for listing activities was spent. Available funding and the number of court ordered listing actions the Service must complete this year limits the number of new species that can be proposed for listing this fiscal year.

Significant progress has been made in recovery actions for listed species. Eighty percent of all listed species have approved recovery plans, up from 70 percent in FY 1999. It is the Service's policy to have recovery plans completed 30 months after final listing and, as a

Goodings Onion

USFWS Photo

result, new recovery plans are being prepared for the more than 75 species listed in FY 1998 and FY 1999.

In FY 2000, the Service greatly expanded its recovery partnerships with states, tribes, counties, organizations, universities, zoos and aquaria, corporations, and private landowners. For example, a new national partnership was created with the Center for Plant Conservation through a Memorandum of Understanding that will enhance the recovery of listed plants. A consortium of 29 botanical gardens and arboreta throughout the U.S. supports the Center and is the only national organization dedicated exclusively to conserving rare U.S. plants.

With its partners, Federal, State, and local government agencies, Tribal governments, industry, universities, conservation groups, and interested individuals, the Service evaluated the current status and population trends of imperiled native fishes and conducted 130 projects in 25 ecosystems involving 65 imperiled aquatic species in FY 2000. Common goals and mutual benefits resulting from native fish conservation were identified and put into action. For example, the Grand Portage Tribe and the Service conducted a telemetry study of the imperiled coaster brook trout movement in Lake Superior and identified critical lakeshore habitats that are and will continue to be important to coaster brook trout restoration. Also, the Service conducted studies on the Tombigbee River in Alabama to restore Gulf race striped bass, the threatened Gulf Sturgeon, Alabama shad, paddlefish, river redhorse, and other native species. Recommendations from this study will assist the Corps of Engineers in their operation of the Coffeeville Lock and Dam, which could help restore approximately 97 river miles of historic habitat. Further, the Service monitored the presence and distribution of endangered winter run and threatened spring run Chinook salmon in the Sacramento/San Joaquin Delta and Estuary. Information gathered contribute to water allocation decisions, which are critical to the survival of endangered salmon smolts in the delta.

Service Hatcheries also work with surrogates for listed fish species, developing holding and propagation methods without risk to severely depleted populations and increasingly with imperiled species, often obviating

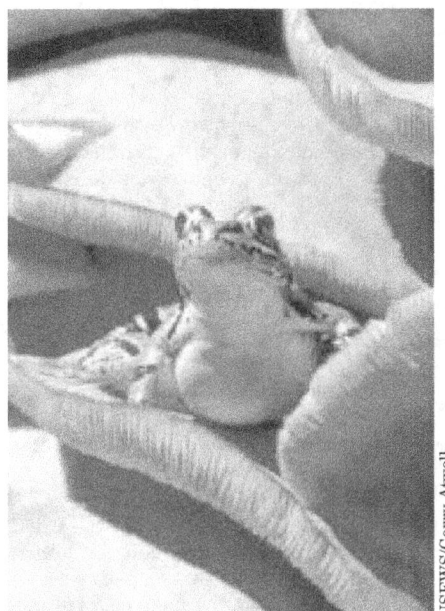

Pickerel Frog

the need for further ESA listings. Restoring depleted native fish not yet federally listed, such as the paddlefish and lake sturgeon strengthens populations before they decline to levels that demand extreme actions. These efforts are conducted in concert with the ecosystem approach and aid in the achievement of Service goals focused on restoring depleted species.

Service Hatcheries are involved in several cooperative ecosystem team projects to recover inland aquatic species other than fish, such as the endangered Wyoming toad, the fat pocketbook pearly mussel, and the Higgins-eye pearly mussel by applying captive propagation technologies and providing refugia. Hatcheries developed and refined culture and refugia techniques for some of the nearly 200 native mussels species listed as endangered, threatened, or of special concern. The Service listed Texas wildrice as an endangered species in 1978, and since 1996 Service Hatcheries have played a crucial role in its conservation. About 200 wildrice plants are kept at the San Marcos National Fish Hatchery and Technology Center and an additional 30 wildrice plants are maintained at Uvalde NFH (TX).

Through implementing recovery actions, the Service and its many cooperators reversed the decline for many listed species. Approximately 40 percent of all species listed for ten years or more now have numbers that are increasing or stable.

Landowners are working with the Service to conserve candidate species and, in return, are receiving regulatory assurances.

In July 2000, the Service proposed to downlist and delist the gray wolf throughout its range in the lower 48 states. This is a significant milestone in the recovery of the gray wolf.

A growing number of species are at the point where they can be delisted or reclassified (downlisted) from endangered to threatened. The Dismal Swamp southeastern shrew and the Aleutian Canada goose were delisted in FY 2000. Species proposed for delisting include the bald eagle, Hoover's wooly star, Gulf Coast population of the brown pelican, Douglas County population of the Columbian white-tailed deer, Tinian Monarch, and northern population of the tidewater goby. In July 2000, the Service proposed to downlist and delist the gray wolf throughout its range in the lower 48 states. This represents a significant milestone in the recovery of the gray wolf.

An increasingly valuable tool is the use of experimental populations to facilitate the reintroduction of listed species to their historic ranges. A proposed rule to establish the seventh experimental population reintroduction for the black-footed ferret, this one on the Cheyenne River Sioux Reservation in South Dakota, was published in July. A new migratory experimental population of whooping cranes was introduced this year. Also, progress was made this year on experimental population designations for restoring the grizzly bear to the Bitterroot Mountains in Idaho and Montana, for improving 16 species of listed freshwater mussels populations in Alabama and 4 species of fishes in the Tellico River, Tennessee.

Black-footed Ferret

Another tool integral to the Service's overall effort to protect and recover endangered species is the Service's law enforcement program. Service agents develop partnerships with conservation groups, State and Federal agencies, and others, to promote a greater understanding of the need for endangered species protection and the consequences of violating related Federal and State laws. Special agents assist in habitat conservation planning and play a major role in evaluating and monitoring incidental take permits to ensure compatibility with current laws and permit holder compliance. Other law enforcement efforts that protect and recover endangered species include increased patrols to deter would-be violators, expanded efforts to detect and prevent the introduction of invasive species, and additional cooperative enforcement ventures to reduce commercial exploitation.

The work of the Service and its cooperators and partners are showing results. Under mission goal 1, Sustaining Fish and Wildlife Populations, and strategic goal 1.2 entitled, "Imperiled Species," the Service set a goal in FY 2000 to stabilize or improve 37 percent of or 197 threatened or endangered species populations listed for a decade or more. The baseline figure for this goal is 532 species. Also, the Service wanted to preclude 15 species in decline from the need for listing under the ESA. To assess whether goals were achieved, the Service proposed the following performance targets for FY 2000: (1) improve or stabilize 197 species listed a decade or more; (2) approve 15 species for removal from candidate or proposed status; (3) remove 10 species from proposed or candidate status as a result of conservation agreements; (4) include 8 species in proposed rules to delist or

Gray Wolf

downlist; (5) include 7 species in final rules to delist or downlist; (6) protect, restore or enhance 3 million total acres under HCPs; and, (7) enhance 300 species by protecting them under HCPs.

The Service exceeded its first and second performance targets by improving or stabilizing 309 species that have been listed for one decade or more and by approving 19 species for removal from candidate or proposed status. The third target was not met because of the time that is required, sometimes up to several years, before an agreement is reached and signed by all parties. Additionally, depending on the biological status of the candidate species, agreements, although useful in improving the conservation of the species, may come about too late and the species may need to be listed. In these cases, the conservation agreement can be the basis for a recovery plan for the species. However, candidate conservation agreements, if implemented early enough in the decline of a species, or used for species that has few threats or threats that are easier to reduce, may result in not needing to list the species. Only 2 and 1 species benefited under the Service's efforts this year for the fourth and fifth targets, respectively. The proposed performance targets for proposed and final rules for downlistings and delisting were not met because three proposed rules for the bald eagle, gray wolf, and brown pelican required extensive policy decisions, coordination, review, and revisions within the Service that affected the timely processing of other rules. Although the Service did not meet its sixth performance target, it still protected,

Striped Bass

Brown Pelican

restored or enhanced over 127 thousand acres this fiscal year, almost reaching the 3 million acre goal for total acres protected, restored or enhanced under HCPs. The Service exceeded its seventh goal by protecting 415 species under HCPs.

The Service works with external partners to protect fish, wildlife and plant resources to prevent their decline before they need the special attention made possible under the ESA. For fisheries, the Service provides scientific expertise and technical assistance to tribes, other Federal agencies, foreign governments, States, and other programs of the Service to develop and implement anadromous fishery management plans. These plans cover such culturally and economically significant species as Pacific and Atlantic salmon, Pacific steelhead trout, American shad, sturgeon, American eel, and striped bass. Service fishery biologists help with restoring fisheries through identifying and protecting crucial fish habitats; monitoring water quality and quantity; repairing degraded habitats; and providing unhampered fish passage. Service biologists assess the abundance, recruitment, and limiting factors of wild fish stocks to establish safe harvest limits, evaluate management strategies, and design hatchery products that contribute to species and habitat restoration.

The Service works with external partners to develop fishery management plans for such significant species as the striped bass.

Another important fishery resource management program helping our partners is the National Broodstock Program, which was established over 25 years ago to ensure the availability of adequate numbers of disease free, genetically distinct strains of trout eggs needed to meet the production needs of the National Fish Hatchery System. The broodstock program hatcheries produced millions of trout eggs that were provided to Service hatcheries, State cooperators, other Federal agencies, research institutions, and universities. These eggs were used by the Service and State cooperators to support critical restoration efforts (i.e., stocking of lake trout in the Great Lakes), meet mitigation responsibilities as the result of Federal water development projects, and provide recreational fishing opportunities for the 50 million people who fish annually.

Within its Federal leadership role, the Service maintains desired strains of broodstocks to meet the restoration and mitigation needs of the different aquatic systems throughout the United States. Approximately 22 different strains of trout including rainbow, brown, brook, lake, and cutthroat are available through the National Broodstock Program. The Service continues to receive requests from State cooperators for additional strains needed to meet specific fishery management needs. Strain Management Plans are being developed for all broodstocks currently held on Service facilities. The plans ensure that all Service broodstocks are properly managed using established guidelines for maintaining genetic integrity.

In addition to freshwater and anadromous species, the Service emphasizes species conservation and protection for marine species. Pursuant to the Marine Mammal Protection Act (MMPA), the Service manages the northern sea otter in Alaska and Washington State, polar bear and Pacific walrus in Alaska, and supports efforts to recover the listed southern sea otter in California and the West Indian manatee in Florida and Puerto Rico. Marine mammal populations are protected and enhanced through enforcement, education, and outreach efforts by Service biologists.

The Service works closely with Canada to obtain information on the management of polar bear populations. Based on an evaluation of new data provided and criteria established under the MMPA, the Service approved two additional populations from which polar bears can be sustainably taken under Canada's polar bear management plan.

Sea otters have benefited from cooperative conservation in FY 2000. As a result of an investigation of a sea otter that was found shot, a reward of $25,000 was offered to anyone knowing about the incident. Also, agents have been working with the California Department of Fish and Game in learning about the loss of sea otters from the results of their necropsy. Service agents provided assistance to the Monterey Bay Aquarium, California Department of Fish and Game, Moss Landing Harbor Master, and other partners in educating boat users about the presence of sea otters and measures they could take to minimize boat strikes of sea otters.

Migratory birds depending on coastal and marine environments are receiving the cooperative attention of the Service and its partners through the U.S. National Shorebird Conservation Plan. This comprehensive plan for the conservation of shorebirds, the product of numerous interagency working groups, was completed in April 2000. It provides the blueprint that will allow Federal and State agencies and non-governmental organizations to implement effective and responsible management strategies that will ensure the long-term conservation of the nation's shorebird resources. In FY 2000

USFWS Photo

Manatee

the Service has 10 active projects where migratory bird biologists are directly involved in conservation activities for shorebirds. These projects include work such as monitoring and surveying at remote Pacific Islands to providing technical assistance to refuges, states, and private landowners.

Another complex problem with managing migratory birds is that birds are lost through colliding with communication towers. Published accounts of birds striking tall, lit structures date back to 1880, with the first detailed long-term studies on tower strikes having begun in 1955. In 1979, the Service estimated bird mortality from tower strikes at 1.3 million, based on 505 tall towers. Today, with at least 50,000 lit towers over 199 ft. tall, conservative estimates put annual mortality at 4-5 million birds and number of species affected are on the rise. Some 350-species of songbirds collide with communication towers. Thrushes, vireos, and warblers apparently are the most vulnerable. There is growing concern with this issue and in FY 2000, 36 members of the Communication Tower Working Group approved the framework for a nationwide research protocol and the statement of work calling for research proposals and budgets for pilot studies. With assistance from non-government partners, the Service anticipates that pilot studies could begin as early as the beginning of the next fiscal year. These pilot studies will provide the base upon which to design solutions to minimize or avoid bird losses.

Sometimes populations must be managed to reduce their numbers because of conflicts with human uses or with human infrastructure. In response to numerous complaints from sport anglers and others regarding conflicts with growing numbers of cormorants, the Service embarked on an effort to develop an Environmental Impact Statement for the double-crested cormorant that will result in a national cormorant management plan. The public scoping phase began November 8, 1999, and ended June 30, 2000, and during that time 12 public meetings were held around the U.S. and about 1,500 written comments were received. Interest is high and the Service is working to complete the draft EIS by early fall. In order to complete the EIS timely, information collection is essential. For example, double-crested cormorants at several colonies in Green Bay, Wisconsin

Forster's Tern with Eggs

USFWS/Rodney Krey

are being banded to determine local movements, migration pathways, wintering areas, and survival rates. This information will allow the Service to better understand the population dynamics of this species and how it may be affected if population control efforts are undertaken in the future.

Overabundance of the mid-continent populations of light geese (lesser snow geese and Ross' geese) is being addressed by the Service and its partners through aggressive actions aimed at reducing their numbers. Action plans are a cooperative effort between federal refuges and state wildlife agencies to increase harvest of snow geese and reduce availability of food to snow geese on federal and state lands. Methods to reduce the availability of food include reforestation, decreased planting of row crops, and decreasing the size of controlled burns to prevent attracting geese. Harvests are increasing through several methods. One initiative involves opening portions of previously closed refuges to hunting of light geese and developing an information network to inform hunters of current locations of light goose flocks is one method. Part of this initiative includes developing, in cooperation with South Dakota Game, Fish and Parks, a brochure for hunters using state wildlife areas and national wildlife refuges. Brochures describe the damage to habitat resulting from overabundance, provide a guide to goose identification, explain hunter ethics and present ideas for hunter safety, and suggest snow goose recipes.

Migratory birds depending on coastal and marine environments are receiving the cooperative attention of the Service and its partners through the U.S. National Shorebird Conservation Plan.

Though agencies aim to be transparent, the public is not always aware of the many steps required to bring sustainable resources to market.

River Otter with Fish

Something as basic as a tag determines whether furbearers, such as the river otter, and...

Another method to reduce populations is by changing hunting regulations and issuing conservation orders that manage population numbers. As a result, the harvest of light geese last year was up 40 percent over previous years. Prior to implementing the special light goose hunting regulations, the harvest of light geese during regular seasons was approximately 600,000 birds. Adding harvests from special regulations and the conservation order to the regular season harvest resulted in a total light goose harvest of over 1 million. Further, the Service authorized additional methods of take, such as electronic calls and unplugged shotguns to increase harvest of light geese during the regular season in the Mississippi and Central Flyways. In addition, States closed other waterfowl and crane seasons in order to implement the special light goose regulations. With these new management tools, the Service expects that total harvest of light geese in the future will once again be over 1 million birds.

International partnerships to protect and conserve fish, wildlife and plants throughout the world are as diverse as domestic partnerships forged to protect and conserve our Nation's resources. Global wildlife conservation relies on international cooperation, education and enforcement at all levels. Not only is the Service advising foreign governments, but also the Service is a catalyst for community conservation action at the individual and local level in foreign nations.

Invasive species stole the headlines in FY 2000 as Americans felt the effects of invasive species in their own back yards. Starlings, brown tree snakes, Killer bees, Asian tiger mosquitoes, kudzu, swamp eels, feral pigs, Asian longhorn beetles, Nile crocodiles, capuchin monkeys, and West Nile virus are all invasive species that have come to this country from somewhere else. These and other invasive species have profoundly impacted every state and ecosystem in the United States. A recent study estimates that invasive cost Americans more than $130 billion per year.

The Service has a vital role to play in preventing the intentional introduction of potentially invasive species, before they are allowed into the country. To this end, the Service is supporting development of a Global Invasive Species Database and Early Warning System by the Global Invasive Species Program

Snowgeese

(GISP), a consortium of the Scientific Committee on Problems of the Environment (SCOPE), the World Conservation Union (IUCN), and the Commonwealth Agricultural Bureau International (CABI). The database and warning system will serve as a new tool, providing ready access to information for dealing with invasive species issues.

Although some plants may be found in the invasives repertoire, many more have served long and well as healing herbs, minimizing ailments ranging from asthma to congestive heart failure. The market for medicinal herbs in the U.S. is worth more than $3 billion and is growing at a rate of about 20 percent per year. At least 175 species of plants native to North America are offered for sale in the non-prescription medicinal market in the U.S; and more than 140 medicinal herbs native to North America have been documented in herbal products and phytomedicines in foreign countries.

Hunting

Dozens and possibly hundreds of these are collected in large quantities from the wild in the United States.

To address the threat of overharvest of native medicinal plants, the Service facilitates the Medicinal Plant Working Group, an organization made up of almost 200 members representing industry, government, academia, Tribes, and environmental organizations that operate under the umbrella of the Plant Conservation Alliance (PCA), a consortium of ten U.S. federal government member agencies and more than 145 non-federal cooperators representing various disciplines of plant conservation. The Medicinal Plant Working Group established a strategic plan and is beginning to take such steps to achieve its objectives. The Working Group is selecting species of concern for each region of the country for which conservation measures will be developed and is providing a list suggested actions that the public can take to help conserve medicinals, such as buying products from cultivated sources.

Sometimes medicines incorporate animal as well as plant materials. The Service pays particular attention to the ingredient list when these animals are protected species such as tigers and rhinoceroses. As a responsibility under the Rhinoceros and Tiger Conservation Act, the Service is developing public outreach efforts to emphasize that trade and sale of tiger products is prohibited. Two public meetings solicited input on a draft outreach plan and sought partners in the traditional Oriental medicine communities to implement it. The meetings were held in New York City and San Francisco, localities with significant numbers of traditional Oriental medicine practitioners and users. As resource pressures increase with increased global trade, the Service expects to be working with many new conservation partners. Outreach to the traditional Oriental medicine community in the U.S. may provide one such opportunity to develop a new partner.

The Service is striving to increase its success stories with the regulated public. For example, the nesting grounds of the threatened spectacled eider have been identified and are better understood because permits allowed scientists to implant transmitters on birds to monitor their movements and migrations. Many programs within the Service, such as Migratory Birds, Law Enforcement, Endangered Species, and International

Affairs, are working together to streamline the process for the public, improve opportunities for partnership and promote customer service both outside and inside the agency.

One important aspect of reform is the Service's proposed policy on General Conservation permits. This proposed policy recognizes scientific and conservation organizations working to conserve protected species as our partners. The policy limits the use of general conservation permits to

American Alligator

non-commercial scientific research and conservation activities, and bases the scope of authorization on the degree of risk to the species and its habitat.

Though government agencies aim to be transparent, the public is not always aware of the many steps required to bring sustainable resources to market. Something as basic as a tag determines whether furbearers (lynx, bobcat, river otter) and American alligator skins are verified as legal and biologically sustainable. The sustainable use of American alligators represents stewardship in action. In cooperation with State partners, the Service has developed a new CITES export program tag that meets CITES requirements for product marking and passes both the durability and ease-of-use test required by resource producers and State wildlife personnel.

...American alligator skins are verified as legal and biologically sustainable.

State and Service cooperation for the sustainable use of American alligators represents stewardship in action.

The Service supports training to strengthen the capacity of communities to manage natural resources in the Special Biosphere Reserve of the Monarch Butterfly in central Mexico.

Partnership does not stop at U.S. borders. Working with partners to build consensus on species conservation proved effective at the 11ᵗʰ Conference of the Parties to CITES (COP). In partnership with Germany, the U.S. submitted a discussion paper on the trade in freshwater turtles and tortoises to Southeast Asia. At the Conference, U.S. delegates participated in a working group on this issue, chaired by Germany and conducted in partnership with the Southeast Asian Parties. A subsequent adoption of a CITES resolution and agreement on holding a workshop on this important conservation issue could not have happened without significant cooperation among these Party nations. Similar cooperation occurred with India and other tiger range states, which resulted in establishing a special law enforcement task force to address the poaching of tigers and illegal sale of tiger parts. As the primary importer of caviar from Caspian Sea sturgeon, the U.S., through the Service, works with caviar exporting countries, such as the Russian Federation and Iran to adopt a uniform labeling system for caviar exports.

International conventions work best when on-the-ground support is provided to range countries for species conservation. This occurs through small grants, such as the Rhinoceros and Tiger Conservation Fund, which provides critical seed money for conservation projects in range countries. One remarkable example of the Fund's commitment to help local people meet species conservation goals may be found in Cambodia, now recovering from more than 30 years of social upheaval and war that have all but destroyed the nation's capacity to conduct research and conservation. As a result, the status of Cambodia's biodiversity and keystone species such as elephant, tiger, and gaur, is unknown. Wide spread trade of endangered species within Cambodia is believed to be due to lack of regulations and government policy on biodiversity conservation; lack of action by local law enforcement authorities due to their limited knowledge; and low salaries, and lack of national and international cooperation. Other contributing factors are absence of hunter participation in wildlife conservation issues and decision-making, local beliefs in magical and medical power of wildlife products, and strong international trade pressure from neighboring countries. In an attempt to assess this trade more accurately, an official of the Cambodian Wildlife Protection Office, as part of his graduate work at the University of Minnesota, conducted a survey of 24 Cambodian

Monarch Butterfly

USFWS Photo

wildlife markets and 12 international checkpoints. He observed eight live wild caught tigers, 36 tiger skins, 5 kg of tiger bone, 6 tiger skulls, 43 tiger canine teeth, more than 50 tiger claws, and 1 tiger penis in trade. His data on where tiger parts are sold, trade routes, and prices paid will be used to generate recommendations to the Government of Cambodia on a conservation strategy to reduce killing and trade of endangered species.

Also this year in Cambodia, the Asian Elephant Conservation Fund, another small-grant fund maintained by the Service, supported two projects on assessing the conservation status of Cambodia's Asian elephants and developing local capacity to insure their long-term survival. Historical information suggests that Cambodia once supported large elephant populations, and preliminary surveys suggest that some 500 to 1,000 elephants may still exist in the wild. Thus Cambodia likely contains the largest single elephant population in Indochina. The Ministry of the Environment and the Ministry of Agriculture, Forestry and Fisheries share responsibility for wildlife conservation in Cambodia. This multilateral collaboration is among the Asian Elephant Conservation Fund, World Wide Fund for Nature, Wildlife Conservation Society, and Fauna and Flora International. Collaboration is helping Cambodian authorities assess elephant numbers, train Cambodian biologists in elephant ecology and monitoring, and develop a National Elephant Management Plan and a Khmer language text in elephant ecology and monitoring.

Although the Service contributes to the conservation of massive species such as the elephant, it also supports conservation of small, fragile species such as the monarch butterfly. This year, the Service supported training workshops to strengthen the capacity of communities to manage resources within the Special Biosphere Reserve of the Monarch Butterfly in central Mexico. The program focused on soil conservation, agro-forestry, and organic gardening. Five communities adopted sustainable agricultural practices as a result of this project, with more than 40 families participating. In addition, peasant promoters are being trained, so as to reach a greater number of communities and increase participation in workshops.

Summer Tanager

Another important program providing environmental education and public outreach is taking place as a result of collaboration between the Service's Wildlife Without Borders (Latin America and the Caribbean program) and the Society of Caribbean Ornithology. Together, they launched an initiative to collaborate with any interested island in the preparation of individualized booklets featuring the common birds of each island. The goal was to produce booklets such as "The Common Birds of the Turks and Caicos," and "The Common Birds of Anguilla," with illustrations and text on well-known island birds. The booklets are intended to stimulate interest and serve as basic primers on island birds rather than definitive guides. Currently, 11 islands are taking part in this educational effort.

The Service's Wildlife Without Borders (Latin America and the Caribbean program) is also an active member of the North American Bird Conservation Initiative, which provides comprehensive bird conservation throughout the Western Hemisphere. The Service joins other Federal agencies to establish effective partnerships and resources. It contributes to this vision by creating training opportunities for biologists in other nations throughout the hemisphere. Training provides local natural resources managers with the tools to manage their respective

The Service joins other agencies and nations in conserving birds in the Western Hemisphere through its Wildlife Without Borders program.

Rufous-crowned Sparrow

Species conservation is intertwined with and dependent on the benefits associated with habitat conservation.

protected areas. Such efforts are critical to improving international monitoring and assessment capabilities and enhancing conservation of migratory birds in other nations.

Conserving Habitat

Accomplishments in species conservation are intertwined with and, in many cases, dependent on the benefits associated with habitat conservation. Because fish and wildlife are mobile, habitat loss, degradation, and fragmentation are key factors affecting fish and wildlife populations. In this subsection, the Service highlights its work with its partners to protect, restore and manage priority habitats in sufficient quality and quantity for the benefit of fish, wildlife and plant species and the healthy ecosystems upon which they depend for survival.

The most visible habitat protection system of the Service, the National Wildlife Refuge System (NWRS), provides a national network of lands and waters that serves as a secure home for fish and wildlife and plants. These refuges provide a lifeline for millions of migratory waterfowl; open spaces for elk, pronghorn, and caribou; and wild niches for the rare and endangered. The National Fish Hatchery System (NFHS) is also part of the Service's land system or habitat base. Together these key systems contribute to the overall success of ecosystem restoration.

Unique among Federal land management entities, the NWRS is the only land management system charged to conserve, restore, and manage habitats for the benefit of fish, wildlife, and plants. The National Wildlife Refuge System Improvement Act of 1997 amended and built upon the National Wildlife Refuge System Administration Act 1966 providing an "Organic Act" for the NWRS. As a first priority, the Refuge Improvement Act requires each refuge to be managed to fulfill the NWRS mission as well as the individual refuge purposes. The Refuge Improvement Act also declares that compatible wildlife-dependent recreational uses are legitimate, appropriate, and priority public uses of the NWRS. There are six wildlife-dependent uses — hunting, fishing, wildlife observation and photography, and environmental education and interpretation — that, when found to be compatible, are to receive enhanced consideration over all other general public uses of the NWRS.

During FY 2000, the Service published its final compatibility regulations and policy, which describe the process for determining whether proposed uses can be considered compatible with refuge purposes. This is one of the most significant regulations and policy delineations affecting management and public use of the NWRS. Compatibility determinations ensure that wildlife

Black-shouldered Kite

conservation is the foremost consideration in decisions on whether to allow proposed uses of refuge resources. Following the direction provided by the Refuge Improvement Act, a variety of refuge public use policies have been revised, including chapters on general guidance on priority wildlife-dependent recreation, interpretation, environmental education, photography, wildlife observation, and hunting and fishing. Additionally, Service policies on concessions, wilderness management, habitat management, and ecological integrity have been revised.

To enhance the educational and partnership goals of the NWRS, new classroom opportunities were provided at 15 units of the NWRS and new Refuge Support Group programs to support expanded community partnerships were implemented. Funding support to hire an additional seven volunteer coordinators was provided at the Upper Mississippi River NWFR, Desert NWR, Texas Chenier Plain NWR Complex, Reelfoot NWR Complex, Rhode Island NWR Complex, Sand Lake NWR, and Arctic NWR. A community Partnerships Grant Program was established through a cooperative effort with the National Fish and Wildlife Foundation to provide matching funds to community partners supporting operations projects on units of the NWRS. Support for current education efforts in 14 refuges was offered and a distance-learning event was developed for elementary schools nationwide via satellite computer linkages.

In FY 2000, a major initiative to commemorate the centennial of the NWRS was officially adopted. Legislation was introduced into the House and Senate establishing a Centennial Commission of distinguished individuals to leverage with partners to carry out the outreach campaign for the NWRS and provide direction for centennial events and programs throughout refuges nationwide. This proposed legislation, the "National Wildlife Refuge System Centennial Act of 2000," also calls for a long-term plan to address major operations, maintenance and construction needs of the NWRS.

On May 25, 2000, the Service published its final refuge planning policy in the Federal Register (65 FR 33892). The new policy establishes requirements and guidance for NWRS planning, including Comprehensive Conservation Plans

Interpretive Display at Sand Lake NWR

(CCPs) and step-down management plans. This policy incorporates the CCP provisions of the National Wildlife Refuge System Administration Act, as amended. Key points addressed in the final policy include basing our management decisions on sound science, and elevating our commitment to maintain and, where appropriate, restore the biological integrity, diversity, and environmental health of each refuge and the NWRS.

The NFHS and its Fisheries Program partners within the Service are integral to achieving the goals of protecting or recovering fish species and restoring their habitat. There are no simple solutions to address the protection and conservation of aquatic species and the ecosystems on which they depend. Though specific threats to aquatic species vary between species and geographic regions, aquatic species imperilment and habitat destruction has a number of common causes. Among these are intensive water resource use associated with impoundments and agriculture; channel modifications and other activities altering hydrologic regimes; pollution by chemical toxicants, nutrient loading, sedimentation, thermal discharges; loss and degradation of in-stream habitat, loss or deleterious modification of adjacent terrestrial components of aquatic ecosystems; and, the establishment of nuisance levels of nonindigenous species. Restoration of

Conservation education is key to community partnerships. The Community Partnerships Grant Program is now available through cooperation with the National Fish and Wildlife Foundation.

degraded or altered habitat is usually the core challenge to the conservation and recovery of aquatic species.

The Service uses the expertise of Fishery Resource and Fish and Wildlife Management Assistance Offices to successfully combat and provide solutions to a variety of aquatic resource problems on National Wildlife Refuges. This partnership ensures a unified approach in conserving aquatic

USFWS Photo

Bass

Restoration of degraded or altered habitat is the core challenge to...

environments for the continuing benefit of the fishery resource, and recreational and subsistence interests. In a broader context, this cooperative management effort benefits large numbers of aquatic and terrestrial species that depend on healthy aquatic ecosystems. The result of this approach has been a greater commitment to conservation through the development and implementation Fishery Management Plans under the umbrella of the Refuge Comprehensive Conservation Plan. For example, the Mid-Columbia River Fishery Resource Office in cooperation with the staff of the Little Pend Orielle NWR, the Forest Service, and the Washington Department of Fish and Wildlife assessed fish habitat availability and monitored the presence and trends of "at risk" anadromous and resident species in tributary streams of the Wenatchee, Entiat, and Methow river basins. Efforts were concentrated on assessing spawning habitat for summer chinook salmon and assessing habitat and populations of the recently listed bull trout. These efforts facilitate the restoration of over 100 miles of tributary habitat.

Also, the Alpena Fishery Resource Office in collaboration with the staff of the Ottawa NWR opened a fish passage structure designed to allow lake use of a newly restored marsh. This project provides benefits to 41 fish species that utilize the refuge.

The Gulf Coast Fishery Resource Office has developed a plan to restore fish passage in the Pearl River system of Louisiana and Mississippi. Located on the Bogue Chitto NWR, this restoration plan will open 200 miles of habitat within the Pearl River that has been blocked by navigation projects. Striped bass, paddlefish, hickory shad, and gulf sturgeon will benefit from the additional habitat.

The Lake Champlain Fishery Resource Office located key nesting and over wintering habitats of the Eastern spiny softshell turtle on the Missisquoi NWR. Biologists believe that there are less than 200 turtles of this species remaining in New England. This project is a cooperative venture involving the Service, the Government of Quebec, and the State of ffermont.

Under mission goal 2, Conserving Habitat Through a Network of Lands and Waters, and strategic goal 2.1 entitled, "Habitat Conservation on Service Lands," the Service set a goal this year to meet the identified habitat needs of Service lands by ensuring that 93,883,301 acres (total acreage managed by FWS) are protected, of which 3,270,333 acres will be restored or enhanced. The Service met this goal this year by increasing the number of acres managed by the Service in the NWRS to 93,962,546 acres, of which 3,287,764 acres were restored or enhanced.

Under this same strategic goal, the Service set a goal to complete 80 percent of contaminated cleanup projects on its lands according to their original schedule. Contaminant cleanup significantly contributes to the Service being able to provide quality habitat for fish and wildlife resources. This goal was met by completing 17 of the 21 scheduled cleanup projects for this year.

The Service will continue to have the NWRS and the NFHS serve as the examples for ecosystem stability in areas throughout the country and as critical tools to ecosystem recovery. But the Service recognizes that these systems cannot do the job alone.

The primary reason for species to be listed under the ESA is the loss of habitat. According to a 1993 study by the Association for Biodiversity Information and The Nature Conservancy, half of listed threatened and endangered species have at least 80 percent of their habitat on private lands. The Service is committed to encouraging private landowners to manage their lands to help stabilize ecosystems, which in turn helps prevent species from declining to the point where protection under the ESA is necessary.

The Service continued to improve the conservation of listed species by expanding the incentives and regulatory assurances provided to non-federal landowners through Safe Harbor agreements. For instance, in July, the Service issued a Safe Harbor permit for the red-cockaded woodpecker in Sussex County, Vrginia that will involve multiple landowners. This agreement joins the existing 44 agreements that currently cover more than 1.4 million acres.

Under Section 6 of the Endangered Species Act, support from the Cooperative Endangered Species Fund is provided to States and territories for species and habitat recovery actions on non-federal lands. This assistance is crucial because most listed species depend on habitats located on State and private lands. Section 6 grants assist States and territories in building partnerships. Grants also provide funding for monitoring delisted species and thus facilitate the transition of authority from the Service to States and territories.

Conservation Grants provide financial assistance to States and territories to implement conservation projects for species at risk. States and territories contribute 25 percent of the estimated program cost of approved projects, or 10 percent when two or more States or territories implement a joint project. Grants reimburse the balance of the estimated program costs. Requests for financial assistance by States and territories for these activities greatly exceed available funds. In FY 2000, more than $23 million was made available to the States for endangered species conservation. Grants have funded such projects as The Florida Marine Turtle Protection Program, Conservation of Endangered Ozark Cave Species and Ecosystems, and Lake Wales Ridge Plants (Florida Department of Agriculture and Consumer Services).

The Habitat Conservation Plan Land Acquisition Program provides monetary resources to acquire lands that complement the goals but do not replace the mitigation responsibilities of approved Habitat Conservation Plans. These acquisitions have important benefits for listed, proposed and candidate species and their ecosystems. Because of their authorities and close working relationships with local governments and landowners, States and territories use Habitat Conservation Plan Land Acquisition Funds to acquire such complementary lands. In FY 2000, at least 12 localities, from California to Wisconsin, benefited with over $14.5 million to supplement habitat conservation efforts throughout the nation.

... the conservation and recovery of aquatic species.

Skate

The Service emphasizes providing private landowners with the tools they need to become full-fledged partners in species conservation. Through the Landowner Incentive Program, Congress authorized funding to provide long-sought financial assistance and incentives to private property owners to conserve listed, proposed and candidate species, along with species that are likely to become candidates in the near future. The Endangered Species Landowner Incentive Program has opened doors, generated the trust of landowners through technical assistance and funding, and leveraged contributions from partners or sources other than the Service. The Landowner Incentive Program is in its second year and has generated high interest. The Service reviewed 138 proposals totaling $15.1 million. Of these, thirty-five proposals, from all Service Regions, were selected

USFWS Photo

Grizzly Bear

work is underway on the reproductive needs of a similar suite of species under different management and physiographic regimes.

In FY 2000, the Service continued to encourage private and public landowners to protect and restore habitat through both Partners for Fish and Wildlife Program and the Coastal Program. Both Programs benefit threatened and endangered species, migratory birds and provide improved habitat or access for anadromous and interjurisdictional fish and other aquatic species. These Programs effectively triple their program capacity by leveraging funds and resources from other partners.

The Partners for Fish and Wildlife Program works specifically with private landowners to provide them with the knowledge and tools to improve the condition of fish and wildlife habitat on their land. The Coastal Program focuses its efforts on restoring and protecting coastal habitats on both private and public lands. The Program is actively involved in projects in 14 high priority coastal watersheds that directly enhance the livability of coastal communities.

for the $5 million in funding provided. Projects include retrofitting fishing gear to protect southern sea otters and short-tailed albatross, fence construction to exclude invasive species impacting habitats for numerous Hawaiian species, and restoration of grassland sites for the Karner blue butterfly and other listed prairie plants and insects.

Tallgrass prairie ecosystems and mixed-grass prairie habitats are important to the conservation of grassland and other migratory birds, which is one of the Partners in Flight Program's highest priorities. In FY 2000 the Service initiated several multi-year studies throughout the nation to address population and habitat concerns for these birds. In Minnesota, the Service, in partnership with USGS, tested the validity of a grassland bird conservation models in the northern tallgrass prairie ecosystem and some mixed-grass prairie habitats. The focus is largely on evaluating the reproduction rates and limiting factors for grassland passerines, including Sprague's Pipit and Baird's Sparrow. Sprague's Pipit populations have steeply declined as grassland habitat has been lost. On some National Wildlife Refuges (J. Clark Salyer and Lostwood, in North Dakota, and Medicine Lake and Bowdoin in Montana)

Through the National Coastal Wetlands Conservation Grants Program, the Service provided resources to protect and restore vital coastal habitats. In FY 2000, the Service funded 25 projects giving 15 States and one territory approximately $12 million in grants for acquisition, restoration, management and enhancement of 6,500 acres of coastal wetlands. In Wisconsin, for example, National Coastal Wetlands Grant funds will help the Department of Natural Resources acquire 150 acres of high quality wetland habitat in Door County. This project, conducted in cooperation with The Nature Conservancy, will provide foraging habitat for the endangered Hine's emerald dragonfly, spawning habitat for Great Lakes fish, and a vital link between existing protected areas.

Landscape approaches to conservation, whether at the individual or local site level or across continents, are essential to conserve important waterfowl habitat and wetlands. Since the inception of the North American Waterfowl Management Plan in 1986, the Service worked with regional, national and international partners to protect and restore habitat throughout the continent for waterfowl and other wildlife that use wetlands. The Joint ffenture partnerships associated

Habitat Restoration Programs Restore and Protect Habitats

The Partners for Fish and Wildlife Program

In 2000, the Partners for Fish and Wildlife Program provided private landowners with technical and financial assistance to protect and restore habitat on their property. In New York, the Partners Program worked with Ducks Unlimited and other partners to restore a variety of habitats including approximately 1,200 acres of wetlands, 1,000 acres of uplands, and 10 miles of riparian and stream habitats. Many of the projects benefit federally listed species including the Indiana bat, Karner blue butterfly, clubshell mussel, and the bog turtle.

Another example of the Program's activities is the Sanibel Island marsh restoration project in southern Florida. With assistance from the Partners Program, the Sanibel-Captiva Conservation Foundation has protected and restored over 325 acres of marsh. Restoration activities included water level management, prescribed burns, judicious use of herbicides, and mechanical removal of the exotic plants. Selective mowing was used to enhance native plant succession and the wetlands were enhanced to extend their use by fish and amphibians and provide foraging habitat for wading birds.

The Partners Program also focuses some of its energies to educate America's youth. In Texas, the Service organized a multi-agency effort to construct an outdoor classroom in Bowie, Texas. Working in cooperation with the science teachers at the Bowie Elementary School and many partners, the Service created two small wetland areas, removed undesirable brush from an existing tall grass native prairie area, and planted stands of native grass for educational purposes. Bluebird and other bird houses have been constructed and disturbed areas have been replanted with native grass and wildflowers.

The Service's Coastal Program

The Coastal Program also provides financial and technical assistance on both private and public lands to restore coastal habitats. One example is the Gulf of Maine's efforts to implement protection and restoration projects that directly benefit Atlantic salmon and other anadromous fish. The Program protected 339 acres and over one mile of A tlantic salmon rearing habitat. In addition, the Program provided fish access to historic spawning grounds by providing funds and technical assistance to remove five dams on the Machias, Narraguagus and Pleasant Rivers. After the dams were removed, the Program assisted in bank stabilization through the use of geotextiles and native plantings. The Gulf of Maine Program supplements these on-the-ground projects with Atlantic salmon research, mapping and outreach activities.

In Michigan, the Great Lakes Coastal Program, working with numerous partners, initiated the Belle Isle Restoration Project. Located in the Detroit River, the project restored an island wetland at Blue Heron Lagoon and a unique lakeplain oak habitat.

On the coast of Maui, the Pacific Islands Coastal Program is restoring two rare coastal pool and lowland dry forest habitats in the Ahihi-Kinau Area Natural Reserve. Through a combination of habitat fencing, native plant establishment, and invasive plant management, the Program is restoring habitat for three endangered plant species, an endangered moth, and several other rare species.

Partners for Fish and Wildlife Poster

USFWS/N Derey

The North American Bird Conservation Initiative will integrate all bird conservation plans with the North American Waterfowl Management Plan.

with the North American Waterfowl Management Plan continue to be the connection to delivering a host of diverse habitat protection and restoration projects, whereby well over 5 million acres of essential and diverse habitat has been protected for the future. Of all the Joint ffentures that exist there are 11 for habitat and 3 for species conservation. In association with Joint ffentures, there are new "all bird" conservation initiatives are being launched in the Northern Rockies, Shortgrass Prairie, Northern Forest, and Southeast Atlantic Coastal environments. North American Joint ffentures are key partnerships that implement the North American Bird Conservation Initiative, an unprecedented alignment of partners within the conservation community and society at large. The NABCI conserves the Nation's and the continent's bird life within a landscape context and is the most ambitious and effective migratory bird conservation coalition ever assembled. Its principal thrust will be to integrate all existing and developing bird conservation plans with the North American Waterfowl Management Plan. Existing plans include the U.S. Shorebird Plan, Northern American Colonial Waterbird Plan and Partners in Flight.

Another tool designed to protect valuable migratory birds and other wildlife habitat across the U.S., Mexico and Canada is the North American Conservation Act (NAWCA). In FY 2000, projects funded under NAWCA standard grants protected or restored nearly 374,000 acres in the U.S. with the aid of more than $26 million in grant funds and over $110 million in partner funds. Through this partnership program, more than 352,000 acres were protected and enhanced in Canada, with grant support exceeding $17 million and partner funds reaching beyond $24 million. Mexican projects typically include education and management plans affecting large biosphere reserves, and nearly 62,000 acres benefited. The NAWCA small grants program affected nearly 12,000 acres. Twenty-two projects were funded with $1 million of grant funds and over $12 million of partner funds.

Protecting habitat for fish and wildlife resources depends on our ability to build strong relationships with our government partners. Through the Consultation Program, the Service works with other Federal, State and local agencies to ensure that activities they undertake or authorize are compatible with species' needs. Each year the Service conducts over 40,000 Federal project reviews and issues some 3,000 biological opinions. The Service continues to use informal and programmatic consultations to streamline and expedite review and identify potential problems during the early stages of project planning. For instance, in Wyoming, the Service and the Bureau of Land Management joined in more than 500 high priority information consultations on livestock grazing permit renewals and transfers through a streamlined process featuring a series of "screens" for potential impacts to listed proposed and candidate species. The cooperative process enabled the Bureau of renew grazing permits before they expired, thereby preventing disruptions to ranchers' livestock grazing operations.

The Service is successfully working with the Pennsylvania Department of Transportation to streamline environmental project reviews and provide protection of important fish and wildlife resources affected by the replacement of over 300 bridges in Pennsylvania. The projects are funded through a $1 billion dollar authorization in the Transportation Equity Act for the 21st Century (TEA-21). To accelerate the

Canada Goose

USFWS/William Sontag

review process, PennDOT, through an interagency memorandum of understanding as provided for in TEA-21, provided funding to the Service to work exclusively on bridge replacement projects. As a result, two endangered mussels (northern riffle shell and the club shell mussels) and other mussels have been protected by relocating the mussels or occasionally, by relocating the bridges. A protocol is being developed to protect the Indiana bat, which is particularly vulnerable to impacts at bridge replacement projects. These cooperative efforts have reduced time delays in implementing bridge replacements and mitigation requirements.

The Service worked cooperatively with the private dam owner and State, Federal and Tribal officials on the removal of the Goldsborough dam in Washington State. The Goldsborough dam will be one of the first dams in the northwest to be removed to help restore traditional salmon runs. The Goldsborough dam, which is 100 feet wide and 14 feet high, no longer serves its purpose for hydroelectric production or water diversion and blocks fish species access to their spawning habitat, bars the return of juvenile salmon and erodes the creek bed making it impassable to fish. The removal of the dam will provide access for chum, coho, cutthroat trout, steelhead and endangered chinook salmon to spawn in most of Goldsborough Creek for the first time in 115 years. Fish that currently spawn below the dam are expected to move farther upstream when the dam is removed. The decision to remove the dam will restore 2,000 feet of streambed and expand opportunities for recreational fishing.

Linking Wildlife and People
The nation's ability to sustain ecosystems, and the natural heritage of fish, wildlife and plant resources within them, will increasingly depend on the public's active participation in the stewardship of these valuable resources. A growing number of the public lack first-hand experience with fish and wildlife resources in their natural setting. Thus, the Service provides environmental education to help the public understand how their well being is linked to the well being of fish, wildlife and plant resources. This environmental information must be made accessible to the public in order to foster their responsible stewardship of these

USFWS/Hollingsworth

Red-winged Blackbird

valuable resources. Also, private citizens, whose voluntary participation in fish and wildlife conservation, have laid a foundation on which the Service operates today and have contributed to the continuing conservation of fish and wildlife resources throughout the world.

An important planning and conservation tool made available to our public and private partners is the ability to locate existing wetlands and other habitat significant to the conservation of fish and wildlife resources. A significant role of the Service's National Wetlands Inventory is to provide the public with wetlands data that can be used by decision makers to support conservation of wetlands and other aquatic habitats. The NWI has made digital wetlands data available to our public and private partners for one million square miles of the surface of the conterminous U.S. and made this data viewable over the Internet. The digital wetlands data also makes it possible to continuously update wetland maps in areas experiencing rapid change. The mapper is a web-based system that allows anyone with an Internet connection to view available digital wetlands data and print custom color maps and acreage reports on desktop printers. There is a link to the Microsoft Terraserver, which allows the user to view an aerial photograph or a map produced by the U.S. Geological Survey for the area displayed. In the first 11 months of operation, the mapper

Protecting habitat for fish and wildlife resources depends on our ability to build strong relationships with our partners to ensure that authorized actions are compatible with species needs.

Notable partners are joining the Service in raising an awareness of the impacts of insufficient resources on...

has allowed Internet users to produce 253,661 custom wetland maps. The mapping program is reaching a broad audience in large numbers, with 84 percent of the users located outside of government service. The wetlands mapper contributes significantly to the goal of providing the public with important natural resource information so that they may become sound stewards. The mapper is available on the NWI web site at *http://wetlands.fws.gov.*

The Service enters into partnerships agreements with a wide variety of the public, as individuals and as organizations, at the national, regional, and local levels to benefit the NWRS and the Nation's wildlife resources. Partnerships bring additional skills and expertise into refuge operations. An important contribution to community partnerships was made by Congress this fiscal year with the passage of the National Wildlife Refuge System ffolunteer and Community Partnership Enhancement Act of 1998 (P.L. 105-242) on October 5, 1998. The Act brings recognition and additional authorities to the Service's volunteer program, including authority to establish a Senior ffolunteer Program, and added support for community partnerships and education programs.

The resources and expertise made available to the Service through partnerships is wide ranging. Notable partners include the National Fish and Wildlife Foundation, the National Wildlife Refuge Association, the

National Audubon Society, the Cooperative Alliance for Refuge Enhancement (CARE), Safari Club International, Ducks Unlimited, Inc., the Outdoor Writers Association, the Student Conservation Association, the American Association of Retired Persons (AARP), and numerous grassroots partners commonly known as Refuge Support (Friends) Groups.

CARE consists of a coalition of sportsmen's and environmental groups seeking to raise awareness of the impacts of insufficient operating funds and the ensuing threat to wildlife conservation and visitor services on national wildlife refuges. This unique support group includes organizations as diverse as The Wilderness Society and the National Rifle Association, and has become an influential voice for the NWRS.

New community-based "Refuge Support Groups" are being developed on a continuing basis nationwide. Groups consist of local citizens who have established community partnerships that support the mission of their hometown national wildlife refuge. Because group memberships are derived from private citizens in communities across the nation, the NWRS is supported by a growing constituency, which reflects a rich diversity of wildlife conservation interests. This wealth of ideas, skills, talents, and expertise being woven into friends groups will both strengthen and enrich the NWRS.

The National Audubon Society continues its support through local support groups, called Audubon Refuge Keepers (ARK), which are involved in all aspects of refuge enhancement, from habitat restoration to environmental education. More than 75 ARK groups have been established to assist local refuges. The ARK program is an integral part of Audubon's Wildlife Refuge Campaign, which works to build a broader nationwide understanding and appreciation for the NWRS.

Cooperating Associations are nonprofit partner corporations, which receive authorization through the National Wildlife Refuge System Administration Act of 1966 and the Refuge Recreation Act of 1962, as amended. Cooperating Associations work with the Service to create, produce and sell educational publications, maps, visual aids, and natural resource related articles, and services. These interpretive and educational materials and services

USFWS/F. Eugene Hester

Hunting

enhance visitor understanding of the natural, cultural, and recreational resources of the area as well as the mission of the Service. Sales from bookstores, managed and operated by Cooperating Associations, help fund many of the Service's interpretive, educational, recreational and biological initiatives.

The National Fish Hatcheries provide a tremendous variety of outreach programs that promote environmental awareness and involve the public in aquatic resource stewardship and fishery management. Visitors are attracted by the opportunities that National Fish Hatcheries provide in aquatic education, including outdoor laboratories and education centers. Also, the Service produces and disseminates newsletters and boaters' guides to teachers and students so they can directly participate in aquatic resource conservation. The ages of the students span almost 20 years, beginning with pre-school children from daycare centers and ending with graduate students from major colleges and universities.

Service Fisheries facilities are linked to many secondary schools, colleges and universities through formal cooperative programs under which undergraduate and graduate students conduct research or work part-time. Under an education program begun in 1994, many of our National Fish Hatcheries initiated cooperative programs with schools to provide instruction in fish biology, aquaculture, fishing, and ecosystem stewardship. Curricula developed include laboratory analysis of fish specimens, principles of applied fisheries management, and hatchery production techniques.

Service Hatcheries also host a variety of special events. For example, fishing derbies and special social gatherings are offered, where visitors have opportunities to learn about aquatic resources and to participate in programs designed to strengthen public awareness of the importance of caring for fishery resources. The Fisheries Program actively supports national Fishing Week, an annual activity designed for outreach purposes. Fishing clinics, display aquariums, demonstrations, and environmental education sessions are highlights of this event. These events not only expose children and adults to the joys of recreational fishing, but also illustrate the importance of a quality environment necessary to provide these opportunities.

The Adopt-A-Salmon Family is an extremely effective outreach program involving thousands of students annually. As part of this program, students assist with raising and releasing salmon fry into local rivers and learn about human impacts on watersheds. The students develop a watershed stewardship ethic and an appreciation for the complexities of anadromous fish restoration.

Fishing

Fisheries outreach often targets boaters and anglers. Aquatic nuisance species (ANS) can have a devastating impact on native ecosystems. The Serviced attends State and national boating and sport fishing shows to educate boaters about the importance of cleaning their boats before they are transferred from one body of water to another. One of the major pathways for the spread of ANS is through the transfer of boats and related equipment from infested to uninfested waters. Also, the Service uses these opportunities to educate about lead sinkers and to encourage them not to use lead sinkers, because, if ingested, lead sinkers cause mortalities in waterfowl.

Hatcheries also provide wonderful opportunities for adults and children to commune with nature. Hundreds of thousands of visitors, especially parents and grandparents who want their youngsters to better appreciate fish and fishing, come simply to see fish firsthand. To encourage these experiences, many Service hatcheries have aquaria, special windows and stations where visitors can see several kinds of fishes, and various displays that explain the importance of being good stewards of our Nation's aquatic resources.

... conservation and on the ability of visitors to enjoy fish and wildlife.

USFWS/Hollingsworth

Bike Trail visit at San Francisco Bay NWR

Facility condition plays an important role in providing the public access to the valuable fish, wildlife and plant resources protected within the NWRS and the NFHS and proper maintenance of Service facilities is a major concern of the Service. Refuge water management facilities, fish hatcheries, visitor centers, buildings, roads, dikes, dams, bridges, and other facilities represent a major investment by the American people in resources that support the mission of the Service.

The deferred maintenance estimate for facilities in the NWRS is approximately $623 million, plus or minus 15 percent, placing the estimate within a range of approximately $530 million to $716 million. The deferred maintenance estimate for facilities within the NFHS is approximately $280 million, plus or minus 15 percent, placing the estimate within a range of approximately $238 million to $322 million. Based on condition assessment survey of maintenance needs of Service facilities, the estimates that deferred maintenance for aggregate facilities within both systems is estimated at approximately $903 million, plus or minus 15 percent, placing the range between approximately $768 million and $1 billion for all facilities under the jurisdiction of the Service. The Service recognizes that estimating deferred maintenance requires the professional judgment of numerous site managers gathering information from multiple sources. These estimates can represent average costs among several sources or can be the costs of the last estimate increased over time to accommodate inflation since the last estimate. Each method is acceptable; however, estimates may vary by 15 percent above or below any discrete number provided.

Under mission goal three, linking wildlife and people through fostering public use and enjoyment of fish and wildlife resources, and strategic goal 3.1 entitled, "Public Use and Enjoyment," the Service set a goal to increase interpretive, educational and recreational visits to units of the NWRS and the NFHS. For FY 2000, the Service worked to increase visits by 2 percent over that achieved in FY 1999, setting the goal at approximately 37.5 million visits. The Service exceeded this goal with the number of visits recorded at approximately 38 million.

The Service's estimates of deferred maintenance are aggregate estimates for all facilities and for all property related to facility operations. The aggregate estimates do not include construction of facilities not previously existing, or significant expansion of existing facilities, or major upgrades of structures, but rather are estimates of bringing existing facilities into a functional or acceptable operating condition. Maintenance of a minor, custodial nature, including grass mowing, snow removal, grounds maintenance, routine equipment servicing (excluding preventive maintenance), and janitorial services are not included in the Service's estimate. Equipment replacement is also excluded from this estimate.

A standard measure of condition for facilities is a ratio of the estimates of deferred maintenance needs to the replacement value of such facilities, known as the Facilities Condition Index (FCI), which is a commonly used industry measure of condition. Estimates of deferred maintenance needs represent those field station maintenance needs that have not been funded for at least one year. The replacement value is the estimate for replacing these facilities at today's costs. The FCI illustrates the percentage of its capital amount that an institution would have to spend to eliminate the deferred maintenance. If the ratio of accumulated deferred maintenance estimate to replacement value is from 0 percent to 5 percent, the condition of the facilities is considered as "good." If the ratio is greater than 5 percent but less than 10 percent, the condition is considered as "fair" and if the ratio is 10 percent or greater, then condition is considered "poor." The replacement value for facilities within the NWRS is estimated at $5.4 billion and for the NFHS at $889

million, with a combined total of almost $6.3 billion. Based on condition assessment surveys conducted by the Service, the FCI for facilities within the NWRS is estimated at approximately 12.2 percent and for the NFHS at approximately 31 percent, with a combined FCI for all Service facilities estimated at approximately 15 percent. Therefore, the overall condition of Service facilities is "poor."

The Service has a proud tradition of working with its partners throughout the Nation and the world to effect solutions that benefit fish and wildlife resources and the habitat upon which they depend for survival. During FY 2000, as with every other year before, the Service has enjoyed the increasing support of the Congress, the President, and the American public so that we can all work to benefit our natural heritage and the world's fish and wildlife resources. We look forward to continuing to build new and nurture existing cooperative programs so that fish and wildlife management remains a useful and productive tool in conserving our valued fish and wildlife resources for future generations.

The Service exceeded its goal to increase interpretive, educational and recreational visits to refuges.

Volunteer at Chincoteague NWR

USFWS/Hollingworth

Stewardship

Stewardship Assets

By law and treaty, the Service has national and international management and law enforcement responsibilities for migratory birds, threatened and endangered species, fisheries and many marine mammals. Also, the Service assists State and Tribal governments and other Federal agencies in protecting America's fish and wildlife resources. Further, the Service manages over 93 million acres in the National Wildlife Refuge System (NWRS) and the National Fish Hatchery System (NFHS). These lands and the fish and wildlife resources they support are valued for their environmental and cultural resources, for their educational and scientific benefits, for their recreational and scenic values, and for the revenue they provide to the Federal Government, States, and Counties.

Stewardship Lands

Stewardship Lands and Facilities and Their Locations

The Service manages land in all 50 States, some of the Pacific Islands, the U.S. Virgin Islands, Guam, and Puerto Rico. Over 80 percent of the acreage of the Service's land holdings are in Alaska. Lands within the NWRS include 530 refuge units, over 200 Waterfowl Production Areas, and 50 Coordination Areas. Lands and facilities within the NFHS are comprised of 67 National Fish Hatcheries (including a Historic National Fish Hatchery), 7 Fish Technology Centers, 9 Fish Health Centers, located within 34 States. Figure 1 displays the acres owned by the Service for all its land uses. These lands are acquired through a variety of methods such as withdrawal from the public domain, fee title purchase, transfer of jurisdiction, donation, gift, exchange, and partial interest through agreements, easements, and leases. Figure 2 shows the percentage of stewardship lands acquired through these different methods. Lands are purchased through two primary sources of funding, the Migratory Bird Conservation Fund and the Land and Water Conservation Fund.

Uses of Stewardship Lands

Lands managed within the NWRS are used to conserve and manage fish, wildlife and plant resources for the benefit of present and future generations. The habitat protected is as diverse as the wild things living there. Service stewardship lands protect tundra, grasslands, deserts, forests, rivers, marshes, swamps, and remote islands — virtually every type of habitat and landscape found in the United States. The fish, wildlife and plants that live on refuges are the heritage of a wild America that was, and is. The Service watches over 700 species of birds, 220 species of mammals, 250 reptile and amphibian species, more than 1,000 species of fish, and countless species of invertebrates and plants. They come as flocks, herds, coveys, gaggles, schools, pairs and loners. Nearly 260 threatened and endangered species are found on Service lands, and it is on refuges and on hatcheries that they often begin their recovery and hold their own against extinction. The Service protects, restores, and manages this fish, wildlife, plant, land, and water heritage. We count it, study it, band it, mark it, and reintroduce it and we let wildlife come naturally by managing its home and its habitat. On many refuges the Service must restore what was ditched, drained and cleared and actively manage wetlands, grasslands, forests, and to a lesser extent, croplands to provide the variety of habitat needed by diverse fish and wildlife species. Control of invasive and exotic pest plants and animals is essential in order to retain or restore native fish, wildlife, and plants. Over three million acres of NWRS lands are restored and enhanced each year. While the needs of fish and wildlife must come first, refuges welcome those who want to enjoy the natural world, to observe or photograph wildlife, to hunt or to fish, or to study and learn about wildlife and their needs.

Stewardship of the Nation's fishery and aquatic resources, through the NFHS, has been a core responsibility of the Service for over 120 years. Although the

Figure 1

Annual Stewardship Information For The Years Ended September 30, 2000 and 1999
(Acres In Thousands)

	2000		1999	
	Sites	*Acres*	*Sites*	*Acres*
National Wildlife Refuge System:				
National Wildlife Refuges	530	87,790	521	87,627
Coordination Areas	50	197	50	197
Waterfowl Production Areas	201	725	200	715
Total NWRS	781	88,712	771	88,539
Total NFHS	83	12	83	16
Total FWS Lands	**864**	**88,724**	**854**	**88,555**

Figure 2

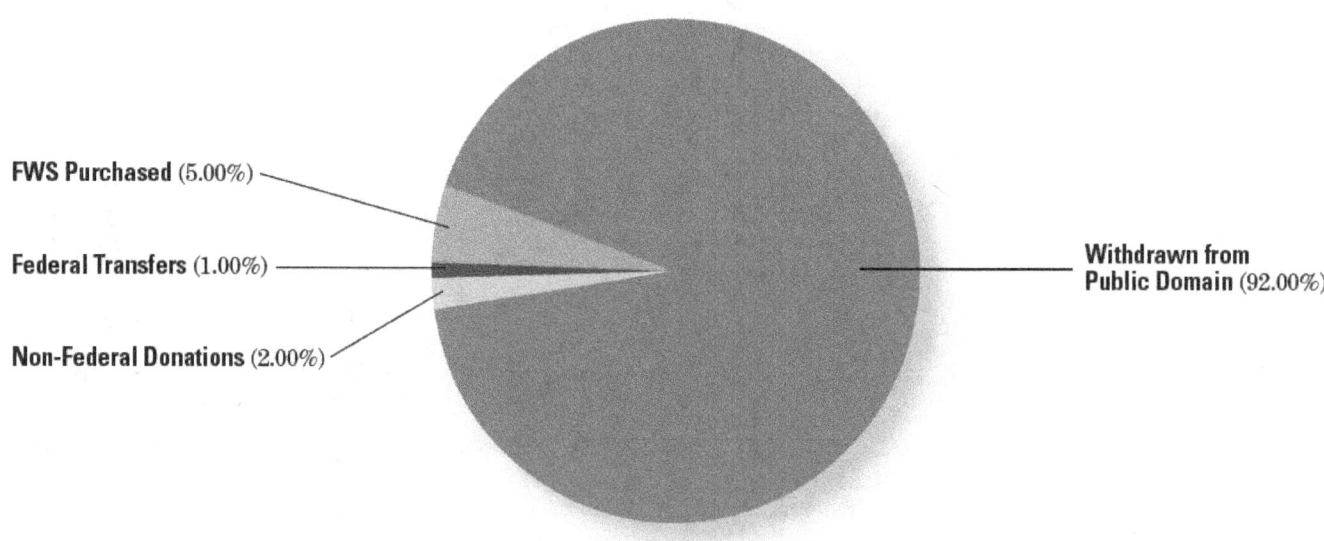

FWS Purchased (5.00%)

Federal Transfers (1.00%)

Non-Federal Donations (2.00%)

Withdrawn from Public Domain (92.00%)

Service does not own all the lands and facilities in the NFHS, the Service participates in managing units within the NFHS, which is comprised of National Fish Hatcheries, Fish Health Centers, and Fish Technology Centers. Many of our hatcheries serve as outdoor laboratories for school groups, environmental organizations, and universities. Visitor Centers on many hatcheries provide public education opportunities for the approximately three million visitors each year. Fish Health Centers focus on cooperative work conducted by Federal, State and Tribal fishery managers to identify and control fish pathogens and diseases, particularly in wild stocks. Fish Technology Centers emphasize scientific management of fish stocks and aquatic communities by improving technologies in fish propagation, broodstock management, stock assessment, and aquaculture. NFHS lands also provide refugia, technology development and captive propagation for over 30 species of threatened and endangered plants and animals, from Texas wild rice to Wyoming toads to Ozark cavefish. In addition to conservation, restoration, and management of fish and wildlife resources and their habitats, the NFHS provides recreational opportunities to the public, such as fishing, hiking, and bird watching.

All programs contributing to stewardship actions on Service lands are tied to supporting the Service's mission — 'working with others to conserve, protect and enhance fish, wildlife, and plants and their habitats for the continuing benefit of the American people.' The Service also recognizes the role that our Federal, State, Tribal, and private partners play in building on the successes realized by the Service in conserving stewardship resources.

Revenue from Stewardship Assets
The Recreation Fee Demonstration Program continues to be a highly successful endeavor for the participating units of the NWRS. Several new sites were added in FY 2000, including Big Oaks National Wildlife Refuge in Indiana, one of our newest refuges. The participating sites collected over $3 million, with at least 80 percent of that returning to the refuges that collected it. Refuges use these funds to enhance visitor experiences and improve visitor services through restoring and maintaining trails, developing interpretive programs, improving signs, and creating accessible wildlife observation platforms.

Also, the Service makes payments to counties in which Service lands and holdings are located. Funding for these payments is derived from a combination of annual appropriations and revenues generated through the sale of products from Service lands incidental to habitat management, such as timber and oil and gas receipts. Payments to counties in FY 2000 totaled over $16.4 million, which is approximately 58 percent of full entitlement.

The Service's Federal Aid in Sport Fish Restoration and the Federal Aid in Wildlife Restoration Programs are the mainstays of State fish and wildlife resource management efforts. Excise taxes, collected from manufacturers of equipment used in hunting and fishing, sport shooting on ranges, and on motorboat fuels, are deposited into a trust fund and Treasury account for investment and then, after appropriate deductions, are apportioned to each State. In FY 2000 apportionments of Sport Fish and Wildlife Restoration funding for the States totaled $434,106,544. The last 5-year average apportionment to the States is over $176 million for wildlife and more than $239 million for sport fish restoration. Also in FY 2000, $6 million was made available for the National Outreach and Communications Program authorized by the Transportation Equity Act for the 21st Century enacted in 1998. This law provides the 30 million anglers and 78 million boaters of America with additional resources through FY 2003 for sport fisheries management and

America's National Wildlife Refuges...

where wildlife comes naturally!

Stewardship of the Nation's fish and wildlife resources has been a core responsibility of the Service for over 120 years.

restoration. This is not a gift from Congress, but rather is the model "user-pays, user-benefits" program. Users contribute through revenues collected from motorboat and small engine fuels taxes and excise taxes on fishing tackle, electric trolling motors, flasher-type sonar fish finders, and import duties on fishing tackle and pleasure boats.

Net Change in Stewardship Land Acreage from 1999 to 2000
The Service acquired fee title or other interests in nearly 325,710 acres of stewardship lands. These lands provide permanent protection for valuable wetland, riparian, coastal and upland habitat for fish, wildlife and plant species, including threatened and endangered species.

The Service increased the number of units to the National Wildlife Refuge System in FY 2000 from 521 in FY 1999 to 530 in FY 2000. Six new refuges were established — the Big Oaks NWR in Indiana, Cat Island NWR in Louisiana, Guadalupe-Nipomo Dunes NWR in California, North Dakota Wildlife Management Area in North Dakota, the Northern Tallgrass Prairie NWR in Minnesota, and the John W. and Louise Seier NWR in Nebraska. In addition, the individual satellite units that were previously known as the Mark Twain NWR became four individual refuges in FY 2000 (the Port Louisa NWR in Iowa and Illinois; and the Great River NWR,

the Two Rivers NWR and the Middle Mississippi River NWR all located in Missouri and Illinois).

The Big Oaks Oaks NWR was established on the site of the Department of the Army's former Jefferson Proving Ground near Madison, Indiana. The Service will operate the refuge through a 25-year real estate permit with the Army retaining ownership of the land. The Big Oaks NWR provides habitat for 120 species of breeding birds, the Federally endangered Indiana bat and 41 species of fish. It is also home to white-tailed deer, wild turkey, river otters and coyotes. The Indiana Department of Natural Resources has identified 46 rare species of plants on the site.

The new Cat Island NWR in the West Feliciana Parish, Louisiana, was established with the acquisition of a 632-acre tract from the Louisiana Nature Conservancy. This refuge is unique in that it has the national champion bald cypress tree located within the boundary and is along an unlevied portion of the Mississippi River.

The Guadalupe-Nipomo Dunes NWR was established with a donation from The Nature Conservancy. TNC purchased it with grant money from the California Coastal Conservancy to protect a rare, and relatively intact ecosystem. More than 200 species of

Bald Eagle and FWS Refuge Employee

Red-tailed Hawk, Bosque Del Apache NWR

migratory and resident birds use the refuge and surrounding areas and over a million whimbrels are found in the area. Other species include the coast garter snake, Western fence lizard and Pacific western big-eared bat. The Western snowy plover, California least tern and southern sea otter are among other federally listed endangered and threatened species that use the refuge.

A new wildlife management area, the North Dakota WMA, was established to restore and protect critical tallgrass prairie habitat in eastern North Dakota, primarily through the purchase of easements from willing sellers. Native tallgrass prairie is one of the most endangered and fragmented forms of wildlife habitat in North America. Ninety-nine percent of the original prairie is gone from this Region.

The Northern Tallgrass Prairie NWR was established to preserve and restore the northern tallgrass prairie and associated habitat throughout various locations in western Minnesota and northwestern Iowa. These lands are the only remaining cover available to grassland-dependent wildlife in a predominantly agricultural area. Eleven species of wildlife and plants found in the project area are federally listed under the Endangered Species Act.

The John W. and Louise Seier NWR was established in Rock County, Nebraska, through a donation by the Johnnie Seier, Inc. Trust. The refuge is made up of predominately upland sandhill prairie,

and temporary and seasonal wetlands. It provides important habitat for all sandhill species of resident wildlife, as well as nesting habitat and migration resting sites for waterfowl, neotropical birds, shorebirds and wading birds.

Through these new additions to the NWRS, the Service is committed to the preservation of biodiversity and the management of resources on an ecosystem basis. Land acquisition and balancing of NWRS and the NFHS resources are important tools used by the Service for attaining these goals.

Condition of Stewardship Lands
The Service has stewardship responsibilities for the lands and associated heritage assets under its jurisdiction, which are intertwined with the condition of the fish, wildlife and plant resources that depend on Service stewardship assets for their well-being and, in some cases, their survival. Service resources are managed or maintained in a state or condition so that fish and wildlife resources are conserved and protected for the continuing benefit of Americans and in a manner consistent with the requirements of conservation designations.

Stewardship lands managed by the Service include refuges, fish hatcheries, wilderness areas, National Natural Landmarks, Wild and Scenic Rivers, and other special designations and are used and managed in accordance with the explicit purposes of the statutes authorizing their acquisition or

The fish, wildlife and plants that live on refuges are the heritage of a wild America that was, and is.

Northern Cardinal

Service lands are conservation systems that provide integrated habitat and life support for both resident and migratory populations...

designation and directing their use and management. Lands placed in the land conservation systems managed by the Service are protected into perpetuity as long as they remain in the NWRS and the NFHS. As new acquisitions enter these conservation systems, lands are managed to maintain their natural state, to mitigate adverse effects of actions previously conducted by others, or to enhance existing conditions to improve benefits to fish and wildlife resources. The Service safeguards the stewardship values of the lands it administers through management actions taken on individual refuges and hatcheries; however, such actions are taken in consideration of the needs and purposes of entire conservation systems, the NWRS and the NFHS. The NWRS and the NFHS are conservation systems that provide integrated habitat and life support for both permanent resident populations and for migratory populations needing temporary stopover sites to rest, breed, feed, and to survive nationwide and, in some cases, worldwide seasonal migrations. While some individual units of stewardship lands can be improved at any time during their management cycles, the condition of the stewardship assets as a whole, protected by inclusion in both the NWRS and the NFHS, is sufficient to support the mission of the Service and the statutory purposes for which these conservation systems were authorized.

The Service assesses the condition of its stewardship lands and resources through monitoring habitat characteristics and determining whether management actions are needed to change those characteristics to benefit their usefulness to fish and wildlife resources. For example, the Service monitors habitat condition through assessment studies to determine habitat quality. Based on such studies, the Service may determine that specific management and protection actions are necessary. For example, sites may be restored to improve habitat for identified species or moist soils and wetlands may be managed to improve habitat productivity. New or different integrated pest management practices may be used to benefit stressed refuge resources or law enforcement actions may be increased to prevent potential or discovered illegal use of refuge resources. A wide variety of techniques, such as grazing, haying, prescribed burning, and farming, necessary to meet local and System resource management goals, may be used by the Service to

promote the habitat characteristics necessary to benefit fish and wildlife resources throughout the NWRS and to meet the conservation goals of the Service. Thus, condition of stewardship lands managed by the Service is not in a static state. Land or habitat condition may be changing, either through the imposition of management techniques or through natural stressors or processes acting on those lands. It is the goal of the Service to provide habitat that optimizes the usefulness of stewardship lands to benefit fish and wildlife resources.

Heritage Assets

Some of the Service's stewardship lands fall into the category of heritage assets. Heritage assets are those lands, buildings and structures, and associated resources recognized for their ecological, cultural, historical and scientific importance. Heritage assets also include cultural resources, such as archaeological resources and historic properties, and museum collections derived from lands and facilities managed by the Service.

Heritage assets include those lands managed by the Service that carry overlay or special designations authorized by Congress, the President, the Secretary of the Interior or by conventions of national or international stature. Thus, heritage assets also include Wilderness Areas, Wild and Scenic Rivers, National Natural

Bighorn Sheep

USFWS/F. Eugene Hester

Tundra Swan

Landmarks, and Wetlands of International Importance. Such lands managed by the Service protect valuable natural and cultural resources in every State and a number of U.S. territories and possessions. The protection of these lands benefits not only the Nation's fish and wildlife populations, but helps preserve important elements of our past and cultural diversity. The condition of all lands managed by the Service, including those lands represented by special designations of national or international importance, are discussed in previous paragraphs as well as in this section. Special designations are managed or maintained in a manner that preserves the values that originally qualified these assets for their special designations. The status and condition of cultural resources, museum collections, and facilities defined as heritage assets are discussed below.

Condition of Heritage Asset Facilities
Heritage assets are defined as property, plant and equipment of historical, natural, cultural, educational, or artistic significance. The Service defines those sites and facilities under its administration that have nationally recognized historical or cultural designations as heritage assets. Please refer to the Program Highlights section of this report for details on the deferred maintenance needs of all facilities managed by the Service. From this information, the Service concludes that the infrastructure that supports the

mission work of the Service is suffering from accelerated deterioration. The overall condition of facilities managed by the Service, which includes heritage assets, is found to be in poor condition and in need of repair.

Cultural Resources
Lands managed by the Service are particularly important for protecting significant sites associated with the Nation's prehistory and history. By closely examining their geographic distribution, an obvious pattern unfolds. Service lands are located along major river corridors, coastal areas, or in association with wetlands and North America's migratory bird flyways. Humans have used these same areas for thousands of years for transportation, settlement, and subsistence. Archaeological and historic sites located on these lands contribute important information on changes to habitat and wildlife over time and offer fish and wildlife conservation partnership opportunities with local communities and tribes.

As of FY 2000, the Service documented over 11,000 archaeological and historic sites on a small percentage of its lands and estimates that it is responsible for tens of thousands of additional sites yet to be identified. Cultural properties range in age and type from the Sod House historic ranch on the Malheur NWR, Oregon to early 20th Century military fortifications in the Fort Dade on Egmont Key NWR, Florida to a 10,000 year old archaeological site on a refuge in Tennessee, to a segment of the Lewis and Clark National Historic Trail on the Charles M. Russell NWR, Montana, to the Victorian-era historic buildings on the D.C. Booth Historic Fish Hatchery in South Dakota. Cultural properties managed by the Service reflect our Nation's rich heritage and diversity.

Of the total number of known cultural resources, an estimated 81 sites or districts have been listed in the National Register of Historic Places. The Service also manages 9 National Historic Landmarks designated by the Secretary of the Interior to protect and recognize sites of exceptional importance.

Each Service Regional Office for the field stations under its jurisdiction maintains inventories and records of archaeological and historic sites. Service-wide information on the number and status of archaeological properties is

…needing temporary stopover sites to rest, breed, feed, and survive.

USFWS/F. Eugene Hester

White-tailed Deer

summarized each year for the Secretary of the Interior=s report to Congress required by the Archaeological Resources Protection Act.

The physical condition of cultural resources managed by the Service varies tremendously, depending on location, maintenance, use, and type of resource. While no comprehensive assessment is available, the Service is developing guidance and criteria to begin collecting information. The Service estimates that a minimum of 10 years is required to assess the condition of identified cultural resources under its jurisdiction.

Museum Collections
Service museum collections consist of approximately 2.8 million objects maintained in 150 offices or on loan to over 200 non-Federal repositories for study and long-term care. Collections consist of archaeological materials excavated from Service managed cultural resources; paleontological collections; objects and documents associated with the agency's history; wildlife art; and, wildlife, fisheries, and botanical specimens. Service collections are used for educational and interpretive programs, research on changes to habitat and wildlife, and maintaining the history and traditions of the Service's programs and employees.

In FY 2000, the Service helped sponsor a field school operated by the Museum of the Rockies and the University of California-Berkeley to survey and excavate dinosaur fossils from the Hell

The Service's goal is to provide habitat that optimizes the...

Striper

Creek Formation on the Charles M. Russell National Wildlife Refuge, Montana. The session was part of a five-year program to survey the refuge's world-renowned fossil beds to identify the remains of mammals, invertebrates, dinosaurs and plants. During the field session, a duckbill dinosaur and triceratops were excavated and a new T-Rex skeleton was discovered that will be excavated in 2001. A Discovery Channel film crew was on hand during the excavations to collect footage for a possible television special. Collections from the excavations will be stored at the Museum of the Rockies in Bozeman for study and possible future display.

The Service maintains a collection of artwork at the Academy of Natural Sciences of Philadelphia under a long-term loan agreement. The collection consists of 487 pieces of artwork created by notable painters such as Louis Agassiz Fuertes, Ernest Thompson Seton, and Jay Norwood (Ding) Darling. The artists were commissioned by the Bureau of Biological Survey, a predecessor to the Service, during the late 19th and early 20th centuries to depict various wildlife species and landscapes for use in government publications. Under the agreement, the Academy maintains the collection in a climate controlled and secures storage area to prevent deterioration and loss.

The Service continues to accession new museum collections each year, primarily as a result of the scientifically controlled excavation of archaeological sites on its lands. The overall condition of Service museum collections is adequate to good. Over 82 percent of the Service=s collections are maintained on loan by museums and other institutions. The Service ensures that these collections are safeguarded through compliance with the Secretary of the Interior's curation standards found in 36 CFR 79. Institutions must maintain the appropriate environmental, record-keeping, and security controls in order to qualify for maintaining Federal collections. Loan agreements signed by the Service and institutions create the basis for ensuring the perpetual care of these valuable materials.

Information standards for tracking the location, provenance or origin, and condition of museum collections are addressed by Service policy and data standards released in FY 1998. In an effort to assist field stations in managing their collections, the Service released a new museum property software package for tracking essential information and preparing annual reports. The Service estimates that it will require a minimum of ten years to account fully for its museum collections according to current standards.

Special Designations
The Wilderness Protection Act of 1964 created the National Wilderness Preservation System. Designations ensure that lands in the Wilderness Preservation System are preserved and protected in their natural state. Wilderness is where the earth and its

Eastern Wild Turkey

community of life are untrammeled by human beings and where humans themselves are visitors who do not remain. Of the approximately 104.8 million acres in the Wilderness Preservation System, the Service manages 75 wilderness areas encompassing 20.7 million acres in 26 States. This total represents approximately 20 percent of the National Wilderness Preservation System. These lands and resources are kept in their natural state and protected from man made disturbances and, as such, the condition of these lands is maintained so as to preserve the natural qualities for which they were originally designated. Although mostly located in the Western United States and Alaska, the Service manages a number of wilderness areas in the lower 48 States including two located on the Moosehorn NWR in Maine and the Cabeza Prieta NWR, Arizona.

Almost one third of the Moosehorn National Wildlife Refuge is designated wilderness. Located in Washington County, Maine, Moosehorn is the easternmost national wildlife refuge in the United States. The Wilderness Areas are relatively remote and are islands of undisturbed habitat surrounded by privately owned working forests. The Bertrand E. Smith Natural Forest Plot that boasts 160 acres of mature white pine is within the Baring Wilderness. Besides several types of forested habitats the Wilderness Areas contain two serene lakes, and numerous bogs, streams and beaver flowages. Two small, undisturbed islands in Whiting Bay,

... usefulness of stewardship lands to benefit fish and wildlife resources.

USFWS/Luther Goldman

Cabeza Prieta Wilderness NWR, Arizona

Stewardship lands offer a wealth of...

known as the Birch Islands, are also part of the Edmunds Wilderness Area. Over 220 species of birds use the areas including nesting bald eagles and ospreys, and over 40 species of neotropical migrants. Several of the old gravel roads that once traversed the Wilderness Areas serve as foot trails for the public to gain access to the Wilderness to enjoy its special character and pursue hunting, fishing, and wildlife and wildland appreciation.

The Cabeza Prieta National Wildlife Refuge Wilderness in southwest Arizona features a natural diversity characteristic of the Sonoran Desert Biosphere. For the most part, it remains untouched and untrammeled by human development. Few wild places offer such opportunities for challenge and solitude in the quiet of the desert landscape. Home to desert bighorn sheep, javelinas, Sonoran pronghorn, many reptile species, and the lesser long-nosed bat, the refuge is currently developing its Comprehensive Conservation Plan to guide management for the next 15 years.

Information on wilderness areas is reported for each fiscal year in the Service's Annual Report of Lands Under Control of the U.S. Fish and Wildlife Service. Wilderness areas contribute significantly to the Service's primary mission and to the purposes for which the NWRS was authorized by helping to sustain healthy ecosystems and wildlife habitat.

For a river to be eligible for the National Wild and Scenic Rivers System, it must be in a free flowing condition and it must possess one or more specific value, such as scenic, recreational, geologic, fish and wildlife, historic, cultural, or other similarly unique characteristics worthy of preserving. Wild and Scenic eligibility studies are presented to Congress with a Presidential recommendation, where final designation is decided by Congress. There are 154 rivers containing 178 river segments included in the National Wild and Scenic River System and each mile designated is classified as wild, scenic, or recreational. The total system encompasses approximately 10,931 river miles of which the Service manages segments of eight Wild and Scenic Rivers totaling approximately 1,258 miles in length. These rivers are destined to always run wild and free as long as they remain in the Wild and Scenic Rivers System and, as such, the condition of these lands and waters are maintained so as to preserve the natural qualities for which they were originally designated. For example, the Service manages the designated 80-mile segment of the Ivishak River as part of the Arctic National Wildlife Refuge in Alaska. The Service and the National Park Service jointly manage designated segments of the Niobrara River, where the Service manages that part of the Niobrara River that flows through the Ft. Niobrara National Wildlife Refuge in Nebraska.

National Natural Landmarks are management areas having national significance as sites that exemplify one of a natural region's characteristic biotic or geologic features. Sites must be one of the best-known examples of a unique feature and must be located in the United States or on the Continental Shelf. There are 587 designated natural landmarks throughout the United States, with more than 40 on units of the National Wildlife Refuge System encompassing about 3.5 million acres. Refuge landmarks vary from the meandering resacas of Laguna Atacosa in Texas, part of the Bayside Resaca Landmark, to the urban Tinicum Wildlife Preserve at John Heinz NWR in Pennsylvania. This urban landmark protects the largest remaining freshwater tidal wetland dating back to the first settlements in the region in 1634. Other Service-managed landmarks recognize important ecological or geological features deserving protection and further study. National Natural Landmarks are designated by the

Secretary of the Interior because they possess characteristics of a particular type of natural feature, have not been seriously disturbed by humans, contain diverse or rare natural features, or possess outstanding scientific values and educational opportunities. The condition of these areas are maintained and managed to preserve the natural qualities for which they were originally designated.

Adopted in 1971, in Ramsar, Iran, the Convention on Wetlands of International Importance provides a framework for the conservation of wetlands worldwide. Marsh, fen, peatland, or water C static or flowing; fresh, brackish or salt C even riparian or coastal zones adjacent to wetlands are included in and protected by the Ramsar Convention, embraced by more than 100 nations throughout the world. Ramsar recognizes the special value of 775 Wetlands of International Importance located throughout 93 countries in the World. There are twenty refuges that encompass seventeen United States RAMSAR sites. The importance of the Refuge System in protecting important wetlands was illustrated at the first annual domestic RAMSAR site manager meeting. Seven refuge managers were stars at this meeting, introducing their sites and sharing perspectives on the value, challenges and opportunities in managing sites with high national and international visibility. Discussions ranged from water quantity issues at Ash Meadows NWR in Nevada, to combating invasive species like nutria at Blackwater NWR in Maryland.

The Western Hemisphere Shorebird Network (WHSRN) was created in 1986 to foster international shorebird conservation through partnerships among countries throughout the Americas. Sites are accepted into the WHSRN if they satisfy biological criteria and all owners and stakeholders agree to make a commitment to shorebird conservation. The Service broadly supports the WHSRN. The NWRS boasts an enormous array of shorebird habitats. At present 19 sites are managed within the NWRS, 7 of which hold international status. Sites range throughout the U.S. from Virginia's shores (Eastern Shore NWR) to the California coast (San Francisco Bay NWR).

Wolf Island National Wildlife Refuge, together with Egg Island Bar (owned by the State of Georgia) and Little St. Simmons Island were added to the Western Hemisphere Shorebird Reserve Network in FY 2000. The area is at the terminus of the Altamaha River; a huge watershed that drains over half the State of Georgia. This vast riverine ecosystem pulses with fluctuating water levels concentrating nutrient rich waters at the mouth of the system. This produces shallow waters richly laden with high densities of invertebrates. Red knots use the area as a fall staging area where they feed mainly on dwarf surf clams. This is the only red knot population know to winter in the United States and it is highly likely that most if not all of the population is concentrated in the Reserve during August and September. These birds use the reserve as a roosting feeding and molting area prior to the last leg of their fall migration to the west coast of Florida. The reserve is also wintering grounds for the endangered and threatened piping plover. Winter surveys indicate that over 90 percent of the piping plovers wintering along the coast of Georgia can be found in the Reserve. Recent information has confirmed that the Reserve is wintering grounds for the endangered population of piping plovers from the Great Lakes. Records from 24 banded birds, within the Reserve, have been linked to the endangered Great Lakes population. Large concentrations of horseshoe crabs spawn in the Reserve. The eggs from these spawning events provide an abundant food source and produce an immediate shorebird response.

USFWS Photo

USFWS Photo

... cultural and environmental resources, educational and scientific benefits, and recreational and scenic values.

Financial Statements
Overview of Financial Results of Service Operations

In accordance with the Chief Financial Officers Act of 1990, the Service annually prepares financial statements of position. Accordingly, the following financial statements display the financial position and net cost of operations for the Service during FY 2000.

Analysis of Revenues and Financing Sources
In FY 2000, the Service's total financing sources amounted to $2.282 billion, which is approximately an increase of 32% from the FY 1999 level. The primary financing source for the Service is Congressional appropriations. The Service directly receives appropriated funding to support it's core natural resource programs, such as endangered species and habitat conservation, and operations and maintenance for National Wildlife Refuges and National Fish Hatcheries. In recent years, the Service's appropriations have been increasing significantly. Additionally, the Service receives a considerable amount of funding from other federal agencies through transfers of budget authority. These transfers support important natural resource conservation programs. and have been steadily increasing in recent years.

The Service has a number of other categories of non-exchange revenue. These revenues are restricted for specific purposes by statutes authorizing the revenue source. Therefore, these funds are not used for general operations. Among the types of non-exchange revenues the Service receives are receipts from excise taxes relating to migratory bird hunting activities and interest earned from investments of excise taxes on firearms and ammunition. The Service collects fines and penalties levied by the courts on those apprehended in the illegal possession or trafficking of fish, wildlife and plants. Additionally, the Service is authorized to receive monetary contributions to fund conservation activities.

Deferred Maintenance on Facilities
In order to understand the condition of Service facilities, the Service estimates deferred maintenance needs for the facilities and infrastructure that support the mission work of the Service. Annually, the Service must defer needed maintenance because of inadequately funded maintenance due to insufficient budgets, growth of the infrastructure without commensurate operations and maintenance funding and competition for resources from other management needs. Having to defer repairs, rehabilitation or replacement of facilities and the physical resources fixed to facilities leads to accelerated facility deterioration. Such deterioration of facilities can adversely impact public and employee health and safety, disrupt operations of the Service, and compromise the conservation of fish and wildlife resources.

In this report, the Service discloses a future liability estimated at approximately $903 million, plus or minus 15%, placing our estimate within a range between $768 million to $1 billion for deferred maintenance in both the National Wildlife Refuge and the National Fish Hatchery Systems. These two systems, individually and in the aggregate are in poor condition, as measured by the Facility Condition Index, which is a commonly used industry measurement of facility condition. This estimate indicates that a one-time funding initiative of approximately $903 million would be required to raise the condition of Service operating assets from poor to good. Based on the replacement estimates for existing facilities, the Service would require an annual maintenance budget higher than current or projected levels to maintain these assets in fair or good condition.

The Service estimates the total replacement value of Service operating assets to be at approximately $6.3 billion. Private sector or industry standards suggest that no less than 2% to 4% of the total replacement value of the asset should be expended annually for proper maintenance. Under this guideline, the Service would require an annual maintenance budget of at least $126 million in order to properly maintain the existing infrastructure of the NWRS and the NFHS. New additions to Service infrastructure will require commensurate increases to the maintenance budget of the Service to prevent increases in deferred maintenance.

Currently, Service maintenance budgets are increasing, but are still less than the annual estimated needs to assure that Service operating assets are maintained properly. We estimate that existing Service infrastructure, under accelerated deterioration, will remain in poor condition without significant budgetary resources to improve their condition. As a result of not receiving sufficient operations and maintenance funding, the Service, by default, may consider either closing facilities or reducing public access to these resources, neither of which is a desirable management action by the Service. The Service is working with the Department to secure the resources necessary to meet its goals in the revised 5-Year Strategic Plan and to meet its conservative goals for infrastructure improvements by FY 2003. When met, these conservative goals may help the Service raise the condition of its operating assets from poor to fair.

Equipment Replacement and Repair
Although the estimates for deferred maintenance exclude associated equipment, the Service is tracking equipment needs in much the same manner as facility condition and maintenance. Equipment includes replacement or repair of Anon-fixed or portable physical resources (e.g., heavy equipment, transportation equipment and vehicles, small portable tools, computers and office equipment, and shop, lab, security, communications or other operational equipment). The equipment that the Service tracks are those that need repair, rehabilitation, or replacement to bring them up to acceptable operating condition necessary for the Service to complete its mission and to conserve resources for which the Service has stewardship responsibility. The Service has determined that much of its equipment is in poor condition and, thus, in need of repair, rehabilitation or replacement.

Estimating the equipment backlog for the NWRS and the NFHS requires specifying equipment parameters and seeking competitive prices among differing vendors. As such, estimates may vary by 10% above or below the discrete number provided. However, the Service uses the median number within the range as the best estimate of the existing equipment backlog. The median estimate for the equipment backlog for the NWRS is approximately $208 million and for the NFHS is approximately $25 million, with a combined total of approximately $233 million. As a result of this liability on average, a one-time funding initiative of $233 million would be required to raise the condition of Service operating equipment assets from poor to an acceptable operating condition. Based on historical trends in annual maintenance budgets, the Service would require higher than current projected funds to maintain these assets in operating condition. The equipment backlog is an estimate of replacement cost. Private sector or industry standards suggest that no less than 2% to 4% of the total replacement value of the asset should be expended annually for proper maintenance. Under this guideline, the Service would require an annual equipment maintenance budget of at least $4.66 million in order to properly maintain equipment managed by the Service. New additions to Service infrastructure and staff will require commensurate increases to the maintenance budget of the Service to prevent increases to the equipment replacement and repair backlog.

Environmental Cleanup Liabilities
In the Footnote to the Financial Statements estimating environmental cleanup liabilities, the Service does not include the costs of restoring stewardship values or fish and wildlife resources that are degraded by offsite activities beyond the control of the Service. This determination is required by Technical Release No. 2 of the Accounting and Auditing Policy Committee (AAPC) established to interpret FASAB Standards.

As a result, the Service may have additional future costs associated with restoring stewardship values or fish and wildlife resources that are not estimated or disclosed in this report. Although the Service has legal means by which to seek compensation from polluters for damages to natural resources resulting from exposure to such contaminants, such legal proceedings are costly and time consuming for the Service and for other affected land and resource managers, such as State and local governments. A connection between the polluter as a source of the discovered contaminant and damage to the natural resource from that pollutant must be proven, the damages assessed and quantified, and technical data presented through courts. Also, most cases pursued under such proceedings are usually settled out of court, resulting in an award from the court that is less than the estimated value of the damages to fish and wildlife resources, resulting in restoration that does not fully compensate the American public for lost or damaged natural resources in affected units of the NWRS and the NFHS.

ASSETS

Current Assets

Fund Balance with Treasury (Note 2)	$	898,957
Cash (Note 3)		458
Investments – Treasury Securities (Note 4)		406,237
Accounts Receivable, Net (Note 5)		
With the Public		4,360
Due from Federal Agencies		430,145
Seized and Forfeited Property (Note 7)		628
Total Current Assets		1,740,785

Property, Plant & Equipment, Net of Depreciation

Total Buildings, Structures & Facilities, Net (Note 6)	617,262
Construction in Progress (Note 6)	2,829
Total Equipment, Vehicles & Aircraft, Net (Note 6)	76,817
Total Property, Plant, and Equipment	776,908

Other Assets
Interest Receivable (Note 5)

Due from Federal Agencies	2,978
Advances	1,451
Total Other Assets	4,429

TOTAL ASSETS	$	2,522,122

The accompanying notes are an integral part of this financial statement.

LIABILITIES

Liabilities Covered by Budgetary Resources (Note 8)
    Liabilities to the Public

Accounts Payable	$	50,851
Accrued Payroll and Benefits		22,952
Advances from Others		1,793
Other Deferred Revenue		(2,672)
Other Liabilities		54
Total Liabilities to the Public		72,978

    Liabilities to Federal Agencies

Accounts Payable	13,674
Accrued Payroll and Benefits	5,808
Advances from Others	2,835
Other Deferred Revenue	62,574
Total Liabilities to Federal Agencies	84,891

Total Liabilities Covered by Budgetary Resources	157,869

Liabilities Not Covered by Budgetary Resources (Note 8)

Unfunded Payroll Costs	35,827
Total Actuarial Liabilities	51,949
Other Liabilities	9,069
Environmental Contaminant and Contingent Liabilities	42,000
Total Liabilities Not Covered by Budgetary Resources	138,845

TOTAL LIABILITIES	296,714

NET POSITION

Unexpended Appropriations (Note 9)	380,575
Cumulative Results of Operations	1,844,833

TOTAL NET POSITION	2,225,408

TOTAL LIABILITIES AND NET POSITION	$	2,522,122

The accompanying notes are an integral part of this financial statement.

	Consolidated Total
PROGRAM EXPENSES:	
Operating Expenses	
With Federal Agencies	$ 205,508
With the Public	1,409,557
Total Operating Expenses	1,615,065
Interest Expense	
With the Public	64
Total Interest Expense	64
Depreciation and Amortization	40,177
Bad Debt Expense	(22)
Expenses Not Requiring Budgetary Resources	16,177
Other Gains and Losses	1,169
Total Program Expenses	1,672,630
PROGRAM REVENUES:	
Sale of Goods and Services to Federal Agencies	(72,849)
Sale of Goods and Services to the Public	(11,407)
Total Sale of Goods and Services	(84,256)
Other Revenues	(50,507)
Total Program Revenues	(134,763)
NET COST OF OPERATIONS	**$1,537,867**

The accompanying notes are an integral part of this financial statement.

NET COST OF OPERATIONS...	$(1,537,867)
FINANCING SOURCES	
(Other than Exchange Revenues):	
Appropriations Used...	903,183
Donated Revenue...	1,097
Tax Revenue...	233,776
Interest Revenue..	22,353
Fines and Penalties..	1,603
Imputed Financing Sources (Note10)...	30,232
Other Financing Sources..	29,495
Changes from Financing Sources Other than Exchange Revenues	1,221,739
Transfers In/Out and Other Changes in Equity	
Financing Sources Transferred, Net...	326,307
Other Non_Exchange Revenue...	434
Non-Operating Change (Note 11)...	733,140
Changes from Transfers and Other Changes	1,059,881
NET RESULTS OF OPERATIONS..	743,753
PRIOR PERIOD ADJUSTMENTS (Note 12)...	(29,504)
CHANGE IN NET POSITION FROM OPERATIONS...	714,249
INCREASE (DECREASE) IN UNEXPENDED APPROPRIATIONS.....................................	(724,239)
TOTAL CHANGE IN NET POSITION...	(9,990)
NET POSITION - BEGINNING OF PERIOD..	2,235,398
NET POSITION - END OF PERIOD..	$2,225,408

The accompanying notes are an integral part of this financial statement.

U.S. DEPARTMENT OF THE INTERIOR
U.S. FISH AND WILDLIFE SERVICE
CONSOLIDATED STATEMENT OF BUDGETARY RESOURCES
FOR THE YEAR ENDED SEPTEMBER 30, 2000
(DOLLARS IN THOUSANDS)

	Consolidated Total
BUDGETARY RESOURCES	
Budget Authority	1,575,325
Unobligated Balance - Beginning of Period	717,681
Unobligated Balance - Transfers	(14,931)
Spending Authority From Offsetting Collections	76,998
Downward Adjustments of Prior Year Obligations	(92,410)
Total Budgetary Resources	$2,262,663
STATUS OF BUDGETARY RESOURCES	
Obligations Incurred	$1,834,181
Unobligated Balance, Available - End of Period	425,256
Unobligated Balance, Not Available - End of Period	3,226
Total, Status of Budgetary Resources	2,262,663
OUTLAYS	
Obligations Incurred	1,834,181
Less: Spending Authority From Offsetting Collections	76,998
Downward Adjustments of Prior Year Obligations	127,116
Obligated Balance, Net - Beginning of Period	824,834
Less: Obligated Balance, Net - End of Period	889,071
Total Outlays	$1,565,830

The accompanying notes are an integral part of this financial statement.

OBLIGATIONS AND NONBUDGETARY RESOURCES

Obligations incurred	$1,834,181
Less: Spending authority for offsetting collections and adjustments	(202,683)
Donations not in the budget	203
Imputed financing source	30,232
Transfers-in (out)	34,391
Exchange revenue not in the budget	(916)
Appropriated Revenue	(70,865)
Total Obligations and Nonbudgetary Resources, as Adjusted	1,624,543

RESOURCES THAT DO NOT FUND NET COST OF OPERATIONS

Change in amount of goods, services, and benefits ordered but not yet received or provided	54,043
Financing Sources for Unfunded Costs	(13,541)
Prior period adjustments	29,504
Costs capitalized on the balance sheet	60,575
Total Resources That Do Not Fund Net Cost of Operations	130,581

COSTS THAT DO NOT REQUIRE RESOURCES

Depreciation and amortization	40,177
Loss on disposition of assets	1,170
Bad Debt Expense	7
Other	(85)
Total Costs That Do Not Require Resources	41,269

FINANCING SOURCES YET TO BE PROVIDED	2,636
NET COST OF OPERATIONS	$1,537,867

The accompanying notes are an integral part of this financial statement.

Notes to Principal Financial Statements

Note 1. Summary of Significant Accounting Policies

A. Basis of Presentation

These financial statements have been prepared to report the financial position, net cost of operations, changes in net position, and budgetary resources of the U.S. Fish and Wildlife Service (Service) as required by the Chief Financial Officers Act of 1990 and the Government Management Reform Act of 1994. These consolidated financial statements have been prepared from the books and records of the Service in conformity with generally accepted accounting principles (GAAP). Although a common data source is used, these statements are different from those used to monitor and control budgetary resources. These statements should be read with the realization that they are for a sovereign entity, that unfunded liabilities reported in the financial statements cannot be liquidated without the enactment of an appropriation, and that the payment of all non-contract liabilities can be abrogated by the Government acting in its sovereign capacity.

B. Reporting Entity

The Service is responsible for conserving, protecting, and enhancing fish and wildlife and their habitats for the continuing benefit of the American people.

Authority over money, or other budget authority made available to the Service, is vested in the Director of the Service. The Director is responsible for administrative oversight and policy direction of the Service. Accounts are maintained which restrict the use of money (or other budget authority) to the purposes and time-period for which authorized. These accounts also provide assurance that obligations do not exceed authorized amounts.

The accompanying financial statements have been prepared from the Service's consolidated standard general ledger. The statements include all funds and accounts under the control of the Service as well as allocations from other Federal agency appropriations transferred to the Service under specific legislative

authority. The Service is responsible for maintaining accounts in multiple funds. Overall, there are five separate fund types:

1. *General Funds* — These funds are expenditure accounts used to record financial transactions arising from congressional appropriations or other authorizations to spend general revenues. The principal general funds are:

a. Resource Management

b. Construction

c. Cooperative Endangered Species Conservation

d. National Wildlife Refuge Fund

e. North American Wetlands Conservation Fund

f. Wildlife Conservation and Appreciation Fund

g. Multi-National Species Fund

h. Commercial Salmon Program

2. *Trust Funds* — The Service maintains two trust fund accounts to carry out specific programs under trust agreements and statutes. (1) The Sport Fish Restoration Account makes grants available to States for support projects that restore, conserve, manage, protect, and enhance sport fish resources and coastal wetlands and projects that provide for public use and benefits from sport fish resources. The Service's Sport Fish Restoration Account derives benefits from the Aquatic Resources Trust Fund maintained by the U.S. Department of the Treasury (Treasury), which collects and invests those funds. The Appropriations Act of 1951 authorized amounts equal to revenues credited during the year to be used in the subsequent fiscal year. This is recorded as permanent appropriations to remain available until expended. These statements do not reflect the amounts collected and held by the Treasury in this fiscal year for reporting in subsequent years. (2) The Contributed Fund trust fund receives contributions for projects relating to endangered species recovery, refuge operation and maintenance, research, and others.

3. *Clearing Accounts* — These accounts consist of unclassified transactions when there is a reasonable presumption that the amounts belong to the Federal government. Proceeds from the sale of vehicles are also included in these funds.

4. *Receipt Funds* — These funds arise from the sovereign and regulatory powers unique to the Government. These funds include miscellaneous fines and penalties, administrative fees, interest, and unclaimed monies.

5. *Special Funds* — Collections made into special fund receipt accounts are earmarked by law for a specific purpose, but are not generated from a continuing cycle of operations. Most of these receipts are available immediately. Special fund expenditure accounts record amounts appropriated from special fund receipts, which are used for special programs, as specified by law. The principal special funds are:

a. Land Acquisition (subject to appropriation)

b. Federal Aid/Wildlife Restoration

c. Operation/Maintenance–Quarters

d. Proceeds from Sales–Water Resources Development Projects

e. Migratory Bird Conservation

f. Federal Aid/Fish Restoration

g. North American Wetlands Conservation

h. National Wildlife Refuge

i. Cooperative Endangered Species Conservation (subject to appropriation)

j. Recreational Fee Demonstration Program

k. Lahontan Valley and Pyramid Lake Fish and Wildlife Fund

C. Basis of Accounting

Transactions are recorded on both an accrual accounting basis and a budgetary basis. Under the accrual method, revenues are recognized when earned and expenses are recognized when a liability is incurred, without regard to receipt or payment of cash. Budgetary accounting facilitates compliance with legal constraints and controls over the use of Federal funds.

D. Revenues and Other Financing Sources

The Service receives the majority of the funding needed to support its programs through appropriations. The Service receives annual, multi-year, and no-year appropriations that may be used within statutory limits for operating expenses and capital expenditures (primarily equipment, furniture, and furnishings). Additional amounts are obtained through reimbursements for services provided to public entities and other Federal agencies.

Receipts are recognized as revenues when earned. These revenues may be used to offset the cost of operations at field sites, including overhead costs.

E. Funds with Treasury and Cash

Cash receipts and disbursements are processed by Treasury. The balance with Treasury represents all unexpended balances in Service accounts. The funds with Treasury and cash include appropriated and trust funds, which are available to pay current liabilities and to pay outstanding obligations.

F. Allowance for Doubtful Accounts

An Allowance for Doubtful Accounts is maintained to reflect uncollectible accounts receivable due from the public. The allowance amount is determined based on an average of prior year write-offs and an analysis of outstanding accounts receivable.

G. Investments in U.S. Government Securities

Investments in U.S. Government securities are reported at amortized cost. Discounts are amortized into interest income over the term of the investment. Premiums are amortized against semi-annual interest receipts. It is the intent of the Service to hold investments to maturity. No provision is made for unrealized gains or losses on these securities.

H. Operating Materials and Supplies

Operating materials and supplies consist of items such as lumber, sand, gravel, and other items purchased in large quantities which will be consumed in future operations. Operating materials and supplies are accounted for based on the purchases method. Under this method, operating materials and supplies are expensed when purchased.

I. Land, Property, Plant, and Equipment

The Service defines capitalized equipment as those assets, other than buildings or other structures, which have an estimated useful life of greater than 1 year and an initial acquisition cost exceeding $25,000. Depreciation is recorded using the straight-line method based on the estimated useful life of the respective assets of no more than 10 years.

Capitalized buildings and structures have a cumulative cost of $50,000 or more. Buildings are comprised of service facilities, such as houses, garages, shops, schools, laboratories, and other buildings owned by the Service. Structures and facilities are comprised of service facilities, such as powerhouses and pumping plants, structural and general service facilities systems (drainage system, plumbing system, sewer system, ventilating system, water system, heating system, etc.,), grounds and site improvements (roads and roadways, fences, lawns, shrubbery, parking areas, sidewalks, sprinkler systems, yard drainage systems, yard lighting systems, etc.,), bridges and trestles, dams and dikes, waterways, wells, etc., owned by the Service.

These buildings and structures are used in the operations of wildlife refuges, fish hatcheries, wildlife research centers, fishery research stations, waterfowl production areas, and administrative sites. Capitalized costs include materials, labor, and overhead costs incurred during construction and fees such as attorney and architect and building permits. Depreciation is recorded using the straight-line method based on an estimated useful life of 30 years.

Property is reported in the financial statements based upon legal ownership.

Consistent with the accounting standards for property, plant, and equipment, most lands under the control of the Service are classified as stewardship land and are reported on a separate Supplementary Stewardship Report. However, lands associated with administrative sites are reported on the Balance Sheet.

J. Seized and Forfeited Property

The Service is responsible for safeguarding seized and forfeited property, from the time of seizure through the final disposition of the property. Disposition may include forfeiting the property to the Government, returning the property to the person from whom seized, destruction, sale, donation, or other methods authorized by law. Property for which a legal market exists is reported at appraised value.

Certain types of property may not be legally sold under Service regulations. Such property includes items that consists in whole or in part of migratory birds, bald and golden eagles, endangered or threatened species, marine mammals, and species listed on Appendix I to the Convention on International Trade in Endangered Species to Wild Fauna and Flora. Such property is classified as "Non-Marketable" and has no legal value.

K. Contingencies

Contingent liabilities are recognized based upon the probability of occurrence. Administrative proceedings, legal actions, and pending claims are recognized in the accounting records when the event which may result in a liability is considered probable and may have a material impact upon the operations of the Service.

L. Liabilities

Liabilities represent the amount of monies or other resources that are likely to be paid by the Service as the result of a transaction or event that has already occurred. However, without an appropriation, the Service cannot pay a liability. Liabilities for which an appropriation has not been enacted are therefore classified as unfunded liabilities. There is no certainty that the appropriations will be enacted. The Government, acting in its sovereign capacity, can abrogate non-contract liabilities of the Service.

M. Annual, Sick, and Other Leave

Annual leave is accrued as it is earned. This accrual is reduced as leave is taken. Each year, the balance in the accrued annual leave account is adjusted to reflect current pay rates. To the extent current or prior year appropriations are not available to fund annual leave, future financing sources will be used.

Sick leave and other types of nonvested leave are expensed as taken because they are nonvesting in nature.

N. Retirement Plans

Service employees contribute to the Civil Service Retirement System (CSRS) or the Federal Employees' Retirement

System (FERS), to which the Service makes matching contributions.

Employees hired after December 31, 1983, are automatically covered by FERS. Employees hired prior to January 1, 1984, could elect either FERS or CSRS coverage. FERS offers a savings plan to which the Service automatically contributes 1 percent of pay and matches employee contributions up to an additional 4 percent of basic pay. For most FERS employees, the Service also contributes the employer's matching share for Social Security.

O. Net Position
Net Position consists of unexpended appropriations and cumulative results of operations. Unexpended appropriations represent amounts of budget authority to include unobligated or obligated balances not rescinded or withdrawn.

Effective FY 2000, guidance issued by the Department of the Treasury redefined unexpended appropriations. The unexpended appropriations now include only those appropriations associated with resources received from Treasury's General Fund. Appropriations realized and recorded as budget authority from special receipt revenues that do not flow through Treasury's General Fund are considered part of Cumulative Results of Operations in lieu of Unexpended Appropriations. This required a restatement of the beginning balances in Unexpended Appropriations and Cumulative Results of Operations. Net Position balances generated from other than appropriations from Treasury's General Fund were reclassified from Unexpended Appropriations to Cumulative Results of Operations. A separate line was created on the Statement of Changes in Net Position to record the change.

P. Supplemental Schedules
Supplemental schedules are presented after these notes for clarification and further disclosure.

Note 2. Fund Balance with Treasury
Cash receipts and disbursements are processed by Treasury. The fund balance with Treasury represents all unexpended balances in Service accounts and the right to draw on the Treasury for allowable expenditures. The fund balances with Treasury are comprised of the amounts below (dollars in thousands).

Fund Balances with Treasury as of September 30, 2000:

Service Assets:

Operating Funds	$470,074
Special Receipt Funds	239,469
Unavailable Receipt Funds	176,400
Trust Funds	13,014
Total Service Assets	898,957
Total Fund Balance	**$898,957**

Note 3. Cash
Entity cash consists of $458,400 in petty cash imprest funds.

Note 4. Investments
Investments in non-marketable market-based U.S. Government securities consist of one bill purchased through the Bureau of Public Debt of Treasury. The invested funds consist of excise tax receipts from 14X5029, the Federal Aid in Wildlife Restoration fund. Amortization is recorded using the straight-line method. Outstanding investments in U.S. Government securities are displayed (dollars in thousands) below:

Investments as of September 30, 2000:

	Acquisition Cost	Unamortized Premium/ (Discount)
14X5029	$406,632	$(395)
	$406,632	$(395)

	Net Investments
14X5029	$406,237
	$406,237

Note 5. Accounts Receivable and Interest Receivable
Accounts and interest receivable consist of amounts owed the Service by other Federal agencies and amounts owed by the public. Accounts and interest receivable as of September 30, (dollars in thousands) are displayed below.

Receivable as of September 30, 2000:

	Service Receivables Intragovernmental	With the Public
Accounts Receivable:	$430,145	$4,360
Interest Receivable:	2,931	47
Total	**$433,076**	**$4,407**

Note 6. Property, Plant, and Equipment
Property, plant, and equipment consist of the following (dollars in thousands).

Property, Plant, and Equipment as of September 30, 2000:

	Acquisition Value	Depreciation	Accumulated Net Book Value
Land:	$10,508	$ 0	$10,508
Buildings (Service Life 30 years):	460,318	151,127	309,191
Other Structures (Service Life 30 years):	542,545	244,982	297,563
Subtotal Bldgs, Structures, and Facilities:	1,013,371	396,109	617,262
Construction in Progress:	82,829	0	82,829
Equipment (Service Life NTE 10 years):	185,935	109,118	76,817
Total	**$1,282,135**	**$505,227**	**$776,908**

Note 7. Seized and Forfeited Property
Property seized by or forfeited to the Service is characterized predominately as wildlife and wildlife products. Non-wildlife property, such as guns, ammunition or forensic evidence, can be seized by or forfeited to the Service, but such property does not typify the seized or forfeited property held by the Service.

Seized and forfeited property is identified by FWS law enforcement agents through the specific law enforcement case recorded in the Service's Law Enforcement Management Information System (LEMIS 2000). The Service is updating LEMIS 2000 and is in the process of transferring case files to the newer version of LEMIS 2000 that will be fully implemented in FY 2001.

Seized property is secured in law enforcement offices in accordance with established evidence handling procedures. Forfeited property can be retained for education purposes, added to the Fish and Wildlife Service Forensics Laboratory's standards collection, destroyed, or sent to the Service's Wildlife Property Repository at the Rocky Mountain Arsenal in Denver, Colorado, for ultimate disposition. Forfeited property, including abandoned property that legally can be sold is auctioned and the net proceeds are deposited into the Lacey Act Reward Account. Auctions remove marketable inventory from the Service's property repository, leaving only forfeited property that cannot be sold due to legal restrictions. Sources of legal restrictions include the Endangered Species Act, Migratory Bird Treaty Act, Marine Mammal Protection Act, and the Bald Eagle Protection Act. Since LEMIS 2000 is a case management database, designed to track law enforcement cases, individual seized or forfeited items are tracked by case number. Thus, the number of cases resulting in seizures and forfeitures are reported. Also, any case that resulted in property seizures and ending in property forfeitures during the reporting period are reported as forfeited cases. This alleviates double counting such cases.

The Service does not assign a financial value to, or recognize for purposes of its financial statements, property seized by or forfeited to the Service that cannot be sold due to legal restrictions. Such property is typically wildlife or wildlife parts and can be donated to schools, aquaria, museums, or zoos for education or scientific purposes. Seized or forfeited property that can be sold legally is valued by individual agents based on their best professional estimate, through declarations, or through evaluating fair market value. These marketable property values are entered into the case file in LEMIS 2000 and are reported below.

Seized and forfeited property as of September 30, 2000, are displayed below (number of seizures or forfeitures and dollars in thousands).

Seized and Forfeited Property as of September 30, 2000:

	Number of Seizures	Marketable Value
Seized Property:	599	$2,235
Forfeited Property:	1,127	$628
Property Dispositions:	2,288	$4,605

Note 8. Other Liabilities

A. Other Liabilities Covered by Budgetary Resources
All other liabilities covered by budgetary resources are current liabilities.

Advances are related to reimbursable agreements with public entities and other Federal agencies to protect wildlife resources, to conduct investigations, to conduct wildlife surveys on public lands, and to provide fish migration prior to the construction of new dams.

Deposit funds include stale-dated Government checks (of 1 year or greater), proceeds from the sale of vehicles not applied toward the purchase of new vehicles, and tax withholding.

The unearned revenue relates to property forfeited to the Service.

Other liabilities with the public are an offset to revenue collected for Treasury, which will be returned to the Treasury as required by new procedures for accounting for miscellaneous receipts.

B. Other Liabilities Not Covered by Budgetary Resources
Other liabilities not covered by budgetary resources consist of $35.8 million, which represents the accrued unfunded annual leave of the Service, $9.1 million for the unfunded workman's compensation accrual of the Service, and $51.9 million for the Federal Employees Compensation Act (FECA) actuarial calculation.

Environmental liabilities for the Service are associated with the future costs of remediating hazardous wastes and landfills existing within units of the National Wildlife Refuge System (NWRS) and on National Fish Hatcheries System (NFHS). The Service believes that the future costs of cleaning certain contamination within the NWRS and the NFHS can be reasonably estimated at approximately $42 million. This estimate of future costs covers cleanup of 10 sites and include sites on lands obtained by the Service through donation, acquisition or transfer from other agencies. Cost estimates are based on preliminary investigations of known sites and the expected degree and type of contamination probable at these sites. It does not include sites unknown, sites for which Service responsibility is unclear, sites that have not been investigated, or sites degraded by offsite

activities beyond the control of the Service. Where possible, cost estimates are included for conducting site investigations and for conducting monitoring actions needed to assess the efficacy of cleanup. The Service's methods for estimating these liabilities included quotes from private firms or government agencies that have worked on the sites, projected planning figures based on related projects, and best engineering judgment.

For contingencies that could arise because of litigation or claims, the Service has certain administrative proceedings, legal actions, and claims pending against it. In FY 2000, the Service is involved in three lawsuits and one claim and the future liability for all four cases is at approximately $85 million. The lawsuits involve various plaintiffs seeking damages for alleged "takings" of property rights. The claim involves alleged property damage and personal injuries resulting from an automobile collision with a Service employee. The Service has defenses in all four cases and expects to prevail in or settle the pending cases. Any amounts paid by the Government, which are expected to be substantially less than the amounts sought by the plaintiffs, will be paid out of the Judgment Fund of the U.S. Department of the Treasury, rather than from Service appropriations. In the opinion of the Service management, as well as the Office of the Solicitor, resolution of these proceedings, actions, and claims will not materially affect the financial position, results of operations, or cash flows of the U.S. Fish and Wildlife Service.

Unexpended Appropriations as of September 30, 2000:

Unexpended Appropriations	
Unobligated—Available:	$130,208
Unavailable:	2,822
Undelivered Orders:	247,545
Total Unexpended Appropriations:	$380,575

Note 9. Unexpended Appropriations
Unexpended appropriations are displayed below (dollars in thousands).

Note 10. Imputed Financing Source
Imputed financing sources are amounts equal to the costs that have been incurred by the reporting entity and budgeted by another entity when services are received at less than full cost. The Service recognizes the actuarial present value of pensions and other retirement benefits for its employees' during their active years of service. By recognizing nonbudgetary resources, e.g., the imputed financing source of $30.2 million, the financial statements of the Service reflect the recorded costs that were financed by budgetary resources of the Office of Personnel Management.

Note 11. Non-operating Change
The non-operating change of $733.1 million represents the reclassification of Unexpended Appropriations to Cumulative Results of Operations related to budget authority from special receipt revenues that did not flow through Treasury's General Fund. Because Treasury's guidance redefined unexpended appropriations to include only those appropriations associated with resources received from Treasury's General Fund, appropriations realized and recorded as budget authority from special receipt revenues were reclassified as Cumulative Results of Operations.

Note 12. Prior Period Adjustments
The prior period adjustment figures are displayed below (dollars in thousands).

Prior Period Adjustments as of September 30, 2000:

Correct prior period costs related to property, plant, and equipment which should have been expensed:	$29,504
Total Prior Period Adjustments	$29,504

United States Department of the Interior

OFFICE OF INSPECTOR GENERAL
Washington, D.C. 20240

June 22, 2001

Memorandum

To: Director, U.S. Fish and Wildlife Service

Subject: Independent Auditors Report on the U.S. Fish and Wildlife Service's
           Financial Statements for Fiscal Year 2000 (No. 01-I-410)

We found that the U.S. Fish and Wildlife Service's (FWS) principal financial statements[1]
for fiscal year 2000 were fairly presented in all material respects except for the recorded
balance for the FWS' undelivered orders on the Consolidated Statement of Budgetary
Resources for the fiscal year ended September 30, 2000. We were unable to satisfy
ourselves as to the balance of the undelivered orders account for the fiscal year ended
September 30, 2000 because of a material weakness in the FWS' internal controls over
deobligating undelivered orders in a timely manner. We also identified three other
material weaknesses, two reportable conditions, a weakness in reporting stewardship
investments in the Required Supplementary Stewardship Information, and three instances
of noncompliance with laws and regulations.

Internal Controls

Material Weaknesses. We found material internal control weaknesses in the areas of
undelivered orders, construction-in-progress balances, Federal Aid program grants, and
capitalized equipment reconciliation procedures.

> ➢ **Undelivered Orders.** The FWS has not performed a timely and comprehensive
> review of its undelivered orders account. We estimate that the overstatement in
> undelivered orders was approximately $23.4 million.

> ➢ **Construction-in-Progress Balances.** The FWS' construction-in-progress
> procedures and reconciliation controls need improvement to ensure that errors are
> detected and corrected in a timely manner. We determined that the FWS'
> quarterly and year-end reconciliation efforts have not been timely, effective, or
> complete.

---

[1]The FWS' principal financial statements consist of the Consolidated Statement of Financial Position as of September 30, 2000; the
Consolidated Statement of Net Cost and Consolidated Statement of Changes in Net Position for the fiscal year ended September 30,
2000; and the Consolidated Statement of Budgetary Resources and the Consolidated Statement of Financing for the fiscal year ended
September 30, 2000.

➢ **Federal Aid Program Grants.** The FWS needs to improve reporting processes used by grantees to ensure grantees provide documentation to support costs incurred for Federal Aid Program grants. We determined that the FWS allowed Federal Aid Program grantees to draw down funds without having all grantees periodically submit documentation on costs incurred.

➢ **Capitalized Equipment Reconciliation Procedures.** The FWS' capitalized equipment reconciliation process needs to be more effective. Specifically, the FWS adjusted the capitalized equipment general ledger control account to agree with its capitalized equipment subsidiary ledger without adequately researching why differences occurred.

Reportable Conditions. In addition to these material weaknesses, we identified two reportable conditions in the following areas:

➢ **Capitalized Equipment Transactions.** The FWS needs to improve its procedures for recording capitalized equipment transactions and establish adequate management controls to prevent transactions that should not be capitalized from updating the capital equipment general ledger account. We determined that the FWS had to prepare hundreds of entries to correct the transactions that were improperly recorded in the equipment account throughout the fiscal year.

➢ **Automated Systems Controls.** The FWS' general support systems and major applications did not meet minimum Federal information systems security standards. The FWS has a corrective action plan to address some of these issues. Until the FWS' corrective actions have been implemented, we will continue to report the control weaknesses over the FWS' general support systems and major applications as a reportable condition.

Stewardship. We considered the FWS' internal controls over Required Supplementary Stewardship Information by obtaining an understanding of the FWS' internal controls. Although we do not provide an opinion on such controls, we have applied certain limited procedures, which consisted principally of inquiries of management regarding the methods of measurement and presentation of the Required Supplementary Stewardship information.

➢ **Stewardship Investments.** The FWS did not report on stewardship investments in non-Federal physical property by grantees in fiscal year 2000. In fiscal year 1999, the FWS reported on stewardship investments totaling $191.2 million that were made by grantees for acquiring and improving lands and non-Federal physical property. The FWS' lack of reporting stewardship investments made by grantees in non-Federal physical property represents a departure from the reporting requirements.

2

Compliance With Laws and Regulations

The results of our tests of compliance, exclusive of the Federal Financial Management Improvement Act (FFMIA), disclosed an instance of noncompliance with the following regulation:

> ➢ The FWS is not complying with the Code of Federal Regulations to require that grantees periodically submit financial status reports.

The results of our tests of compliance with the FFMIA disclosed instances of noncompliance with the following regulations:

> ➢ The FWS is not in full compliance with OMB Circular A-130, "Security of Federal Automated Information Resources," to ensure information in automated systems is adequately safeguarded.

> ➢ The FWS is not complying with the Statement of Federal Financial Accounting Standards Number 8 to report stewardship investments made by grantees relating to non-Federal physical property.

Consistency of Other Information

We found that the information presented in the Management Discussion and Analysis Section and the supplementary information sections of the FWS' Annual Report for fiscal year 2000 was consistent with the principal financial statements.

We made 19 recommendations to correct the identified weaknesses. Based on the FWS' response to the draft report (see Appendix 3 of the Independent Auditors Report), we consider 2 of the recommendations unresolved and 17 of the recommendations resolved but not implemented (see Appendix 4 of the Independent Auditors Report). The recommendations that were considered not resolved or implemented will be referred to the Assistant Secretary for Policy, Management and Budget for resolution and tracking of implementation.

Section 5(a) of the Inspector General Act (5 U.S.C. app. 3) requires the Office of Inspector General to list this report in its semiannual report to the Congress. In addition, the Office of Inspector General provides audit reports to the Congress.

3

The attached Independent Auditors' Report is intended for the information of management of the Department of the Interior, the Office of Management and Budget, and the Congress. The report, however, is a matter of public record and its distribution is not limited.

Roger LaRouche

Assistant Inspector General
for Audits

Attachment:
Independent Auditors Report

Independent Auditors Report
U.S. Fish and Wildlife Service
Financial Statements
Fiscal Year 2000

We have audited the U.S. Fish and Wildlife Service's (FWS) principal financial statements for the fiscal year ended September 30, 2000. The FWS' principal financial statements consist of the Consolidated Statement of Financial Position as of September 30, 2000; the Consolidated Statement of Net Cost and Consolidated Statement of Changes in Net Position for the fiscal year ended September 30, 2000; and the Consolidated Statement of Budgetary Resources and the Consolidated Statement of Financing for the fiscal year ended September 30, 2000. These financial statements are the responsibility of the FWS, and our responsibility is to express an opinion, based on our audit, on these principal financial statements.

Except as discussed in the following paragraph our audit was conducted in accordance with the "Government Auditing Standards," issued by the Comptroller General of the United States, and with the Office of Management and Budget (OMB) Bulletin 01-02, "Audit Requirements for Federal Financial Statements." These standards require that we plan and perform the audit to obtain reasonable assurance as to whether the accompanying principal financial statements are free of material misstatement. An audit includes examining, on a test basis, evidence supporting the amounts and disclosures contained in the principal financial statements and the accompanying notes. An audit also includes assessing the accounting principles used and the significant estimates made by management, as well as evaluating the overall financial statements presentation. We believe that our audit work provides a reasonable basis for our opinion. The objective, scope, and methodology of our work are discussed in Appendix 1

5

Opinion on Principal Financial Statements

We were unable to satisfy ourselves as to the recorded balance for the FWS' undelivered orders on the Consolidated Statement of Budgetary Resources for the fiscal year ended September 30, 2000. Nor were we able to satisfy ourselves as to the balance by other auditing procedures. The uncertainty over the September 30, 2000 balance resulted from a material weakness in the FWS' internal controls over deobligating undelivered orders in a timely manner. This weakness is addressed in our report on the FWS' internal controls.

In our opinion, except for the qualification discussed in the preceding paragraph, the principal financial statements audited by us present fairly, in all material respects, the Consolidated Statement of Financial Position as of September 30, 2000; the Consolidated Statement of Net Cost and Consolidated Statement of Changes in Net Position for the fiscal year ended September 30, 2000; and the Consolidated Statement of Budgetary Resources and the Consolidated Statement of Financing for the fiscal year ended September 30, 2000 in conformity with generally accepted accounting principles.

As discussed in Note 11 to the financial statements, the FWS changed its accounting for appropriations of trust and special receipt revenues in accordance with new guidance from the Department of the Treasury.

The FWS has not presented its investment in non-Federal physical assets as required by the Statement of Federal Financial Accounting Standards Number 8, Supplementary Stewardship Reporting. The Federal Accounting Standards Advisory Board has determined this information is necessary to supplement, although not required to be part of, the principal financial statements. This matter is discussed in the Stewardship and Performance Measures section of this report.

Our audit was conducted to form an opinion on the principal financial statements taken as a whole, and our opinion relates only to the principal financial statements. The supplemental financial and management information contained in the FWS' Annual Report is presented for additional analysis and is not a required part of the principal financial statements. We applied certain limited procedures, including discussions with management on the

6

methods of measurement and presentation of this information, to ensure compliance with the OMB guidance and consistency with the financial statements. We found that the management information presented in the FWS' Annual Report is consistent with the principal financial statements. This information, however, has not been subjected to the auditing procedures applied in our audit of the principal financial statements, and accordingly, we express no opinion on it.

Report on Internal Controls

In planning and performing our audit, we considered the FWS' internal controls over financial reporting by obtaining an understanding of the internal controls, determining whether these internal controls had been placed in operation, assessing control risks, and performing tests of controls to determine our auditing procedures for the purpose of expressing an opinion on the principal financial statements. We limited our internal control testing to those controls necessary to achieve the objectives described in Bulletin 01-02. We did not test all internal controls relevant to operating objectives as broadly defined by the Federal Managers' Financial Integrity Act of 1982, such as those controls relevant to ensuring efficient operations. The objective of our audit was not to provide assurance on internal controls, and accordingly, we do not express an opinion on the internal controls.

Our consideration of the internal controls over financial reporting would not necessarily disclose all matters in the internal controls over financial reporting that might be reportable conditions. Under standards issued by the American Institute of Certified Public Accountants, reportable conditions are matters coming to our attention relating to significant deficiencies in the design or operation of the internal controls that, in our judgment, could adversely affect the FWS' ability to record, process, summarize, and report financial data consistent with the assertions made by management in the financial statements. Material weaknesses are reportable conditions in which the design or operation of one or more of the internal control components does not reduce to a relatively low level the risk that misstatements in amounts that would be material in relation to the financial statements being audited may occur and not be detected within a timely period by employees in the normal course of performing their assigned functions. Because of inherent limitations in internal controls, misstatements, losses, or noncompliance may nevertheless occur and not be detected.

7

We did note, however, certain matters involving the internal controls and their operation that we consider to be material weaknesses or reportable conditions.

Material Weaknesses

Our review identified four conditions that we believe to be material weaknesses which are summarized in the paragraphs that follow.

A. Undelivered Orders

The FWS needs to perform timely and comprehensive reviews of its undelivered orders account. Although the regional offices have conducted reviews and, in many cases, have made entries to correct invalid obligations, these reviews were not comprehensive.

During the audit, we also found the following:

➢ The FWS has not provided adequate oversight to ensure that each region reconciles Federal Aid Program grant data in the Federal Aid Information Management Systems (FAIMS) to data in the Federal Financial System (FFS). During fiscal year 2000, the FWS established procedures requiring each region to reconcile the two systems on a monthly basis. This procedure, however, was not uniformly followed. Region 5, for example, submitted only one reconciliation report in 15 months. Further, on February 1, 2001, when the Region submitted the report, it identified 112 reconciling items totaling $17.5 million. (Subsequently, the FWS Finance Center researched the reconciling items in the Region's report and found that there were substantially fewer reconciling items for a lesser amount than originally reported.)

➢ Currently, it takes the National Business Center (NBC), an organization which is contracted to perform fiscal activities for the FWS, from 45 days to 6 months to correct differences in the FFS because:
- Regions were not providing complete and accurate information to the NBC to record the entries in the FFS to correct differences.
- The NBC was not following up with the regions and informing the FWS management when regions did not provide complete documentation.

As a result, we were not able to satisfy ourselves as to the balance of the undelivered orders recorded on the Consolidated Statement of Budgetary Resources for the fiscal year ended September 30,

8

2000. Our review estimated that the most likely error was an overstatement in undelivered orders of $23.4 million.

Recommendations

We recommend that the FWS:

1. Train regional and Division of Finance personnel in regard to undelivered orders, and ensure that the training:
    a. Emphasizes the need for performing periodic reviews of undelivered orders.
    b. Emphasizes the need for retaining workpapers to verify the validity of obligations.
    c. Provides examples that show reasons why obligations may not be valid.

2. Ensure undelivered orders reviews and Federal Aid grant reconciliations are performed in a timely and comprehensive manner.

3. Establish procedures to ensure that the regions report necessary corrections to the undelivered orders balances on a monthly basis.

4. Report a material internal control weakness relating to the FWS' need to improve procedures for performing comprehensive reviews of its undelivered orders account balance in the FWS Fiscal Year 2001 Federal Managers' Financial Integrity Act report to the Department of the Interior unless all corrective actions have been completed by September 30, 2001.

The FWS Response: The FWS agrees with this finding. The FWS is planning on providing (1) additional guidance, with respect to performing undelivered orders reviews, in its year-end closing procedures and (2) training for field level managers and employees.

The FWS plans to strengthen year-end guidance pertaining to the review of undelivered orders. The FWS believes that greater focus on timely reviews of the undelivered orders balance is necessary. For Federal Aid, the FWS conducted a workshop, which reconciled 90 percent of the differences between the Federal Financial System (FFS) and the Federal Aid Information Management System (FAIMS). The remaining 10 percent of the differences will be reconciled by June 30, 2001. The workshop also drafted improved policies and procedures for promptly

9

reconciling discrepancies between the FFS and FAIMS. The FWS will implement a Servicewide quarterly review process for undelivered orders that remain unchanged for a year.

The FWS plans on conducting undelivered orders review training for regional and Division of Finance personnel. The FWS is concerned that the criteria used in the training for assessing the validity of undelivered orders is still being refined and decisions on when to adjust the undelivered orders balance is often subjective. The FWS plans on participating in the Finance Officers' Partnership task group to address undelivered orders issues.

B. Construction-in-Progress Account

The FWS needs to improve its reconciliation procedures for the construction-in-progress account in order to detect and correct errors in a timely manner. In response to our 1999 financial statement audit, the FWS established additional reconciliation procedures to address the problems. We found, however, that the FWS' quarterly and year-end reconciliation efforts have not been timely or complete. As a result, the construction-in-progress general ledger account was overstated. The FWS made adjusting entries to correct the account balance, including transferring:

- $40 million to the buildings account for completed construction projects.
- $34.7 million to the structures account for completed projects.
- $24.2 million to the operating expenses account.

The overstatements have occurred because the FWS has not provided oversight to ensure reconciliations are being done promptly or completely. Additionally, the FWS has not designed procedures to ensure that only costs for capitalized projects are included in the construction-in-progress account. In fact, the FWS uses the construction-in-progress account to record all project costs, including those that it knows will be written off to operating expense. This causes an extensive reconciliation process.

Recommendations

We recommend that the FWS:

1. Develop oversight procedures to ensure that the quarterly reconciliations are performed and reviewed promptly.

2. Implement procedures to ensure that only costs for capital projects are recorded in the construction-in-progress account.

10

3. Report a material internal control weakness relating to the FWS' need to improve its procedures for ensuring accurate construction-in-progress balances in its fiscal year 2001 Federal Managers' Financial Integrity Act report to the Department of the Interior unless the corrective actions are completed by September 30, 2001.

The FWS Response: The FWS agrees with this finding and recommendations. The FWS is developing strengthened guidance for reconciling the construction-in-progress account to the property records. The FWS has committed to perform two construction-in-progress reconciliations per year. The FWS is also investigating system changes to minimize recording expense transactions in the Construction Work-in-Progress account.

The OIG Reply: The FWS' response to investigate rather than investigate and implement system changes to minimize recording expense transactions in the construction-in-progress account does not satisfy the intent of the second recommendation. We therefore consider this recommendation unresolved.

C. Processes Used by Grantees to Document and Support Costs Incurred for Federal Aid Program Grants

The FWS needs to improve reporting processes used by grantees to ensure grantees provide documentation to support costs incurred for Federal Aid Grants. The FWS doesn't require its grantees to submit annual financial status reports. Instead the FWS requires the submission of the financial status report 90 days after the close out of the grant. The FWS needs this information annually to properly reconcile grant expenditures and to ensure the expenses were recorded in the appropriate accounting period. As a result, the FWS had to record a high level adjustment to correct the estimated overstatements in the accounts payable and related accounts. Further, the FWS is not in compliance with 43 CFR 12.81 (b) , which requires grantees to report on the status of funds at least annually.

The Federal Financial Assistance Improvement Act of 1999 requires that agencies implement a system by May 20, 2001 that allows grantees to electronically apply for and report on the use of funds. We found that the FWS was working with the Department and other Federal agencies to develop and implement a system as required. The system, when implemented, should simplify reporting processes for grantees and should provide the necessary support.

11

Recommendations

We recommend that the FWS:

1. Ensure that electronic procedures are implemented to support that grantees cash drawdowns are either for costs that were previously incurred or for advances.

2. As an interim step, require that grantees submit financial status reports annually to comply with 43 CFR 12.81(b). The FWS should then use this information to calculate year-end grant expense accruals.

3. Report a material internal control weakness relating to grantees not providing sufficient documentation to support costs incurred for the FWS' Federal Aid Program grants in its Fiscal Year 2001 Federal Managers' Financial Integrity Act report to the Department of the Interior unless the corrective actions are completed by September 30, 2001.

The FWS Response: The FWS agrees with this finding and will implement electronic processes being developed by the Interagency Electronic Grants Committee (IAEGC) as soon as they are available. The FWS has been working with the Department and other Federal agencies as part of the IAEGC to develop and implement electronic processes to streamline reporting processes for grantees. The actions planned by IAEGC, when implemented, should simplify reporting processes for grantees, streamline reconciliation steps for financial reporting purposes, improve the FWS' financial management practices, and meet OMB reporting requirements.

The FWS will require annual financial status reports from grantees at the end of the grant year. The FWS will not receive financial status reports from the grantees at the end of the fiscal year but will receive the reports on the anniversary dates of the grants. The FWS will select a methodology to calculate year-end grant expense accruals that will satisfy year-end financial reporting requirements.

D. Capitalized Equipment Reconciliation Procedures

The FWS needs to improve its procedures for reconciling capitalized equipment. The FWS adjusted the equipment general ledger control account to agree with its subsidiary ledger without adequately researching why differences occurred. Reconciling items were not adequately researched due to time constraints and the labor-intensive manual processes. There were not enough

12

common data elements in the Federal Financial System and the capital equipment subsidiary system to perform an electronic reconciliation. To bring the general ledger into balance with the subsidiary ledger for fiscal year 2000, the FWS added $8.1 million to the equipment account and reduced its operating expense by the same amount. The FWS also subtracted $4.7 million from the general ledger equipment account and increased its operating expense account by that amount.

Recommendations

We recommend that the FWS:

1. Implement procedures to identify the nature and cause of all differences between the capitalized equipment general ledger control account and the subsidiary ledger prior to making any adjustments.

2. Establish common transaction data elements in the FFS and the capitalized equipment subsidiary system to help ensure that the majority of reconciling items can be reconciled in a timely manner.

3. Report the lack of a capitalized equipment reconciliation between the general and subsidiary ledger as a material internal control weakness in the Fiscal Year 2001 Federal Managers' Financial Integrity Act report to the Department of the Interior unless the corrective actions are completed by September 30, 2001.

The FWS Response: The FWS recognizes the need to improve the accuracy of recording capital equipment transactions and the procedures to reconcile the Federal Financial System and the property systems. The FWS will establish a working group comprised of representatives of Finance and Contracting and General Services personnel to prepare guidelines for identifying and documenting the nature of differences between the equipment general ledger control account and the subsidiary ledger and to establish common transaction data elements for the Federal Financial System and the FWS personal property files. If it is determined that existing systems cannot effectively be modified to include additional common data elements, the FWS will consult with the Department concerning replacement systems.

13

Reportable Conditions

E. Procedures for Recording Capitalized Equipment Transactions

The FWS needs to improve its procedures for recording capitalized equipment transactions. Specifically, the FWS has not trained its staff to properly code non-capital equipment transactions or established controls to prevent recording non-capital equipment in the equipment general ledger. Although the FWS established a reconciliation process to correct these transactions after-the-fact, improvements are needed when the transactions are recorded. The established process resulted in the FWS' need to research and prepare manual voucher entries for 762 transactions to correct the coding errors that occurred throughout fiscal year 2000.

Recommendations

We recommend that the FWS:

1. Ensure that additional training is provided for remote data entry personnel to ensure transactions are properly recorded at the time the transactions are entered into the system.

2. Ensure that front-end computer system edits and controls are designed to ensure that transactions are properly processed at the time the transactions are entered into the system.

The FWS Response: The FWS agrees with this finding. The FWS plans to train personnel to record transactions properly. The training will be based on the procedures and guidance developed by the FWS task force established to address capitalized equipment reconciliation. The FWS task force will also evaluate whether the computer systems can be modified to include front-end edits to ensure transactions are properly recorded. If it is determined that existing systems cannot effectively be modified to include front-end edits and controls, the FWS will consult with the Department concerning replacement systems.

F. FWS Needs Improved General Controls Over Its Automated Systems

The FWS' general support systems and major applications did not meet minimum Federal information systems security standards. Office of Management and Budget Circular A-130, "Management of Federal Information Resources," Appendix III, "Security of Federal Automated Information Resources," requires that adequate security be provided for all agency information collected, processed, transmitted, stored, or disseminated in general support systems and major applications. To ensure information is adequately safeguarded, the FWS needs to:

14

➢ **Appropriately assign responsibility for security.** The FWS regional offices/installations did not have appropriate individuals responsible for information technology security. For example, at Region 2 the responsible official for the Ecological Services' LAN and e-mail server was a biologist even though Region 2 has an IRM official. The FWS has identified numerous information systems security control weaknesses for the Ecological Services' LAN and e-mail server. The standards require that information technology mangers be knowledgeable about information technology security matters. We do not believe that a biologist is the appropriate person to be responsible for correcting these issues or to have the security responsibility for these general support systems. Additionally, FWS identified information system security weaknesses for the Facility Management Information System including the lack of a security officer. In this instance a computer specialist was assigned the responsibility for security. It is an internal control weakness to have a computer specialist who is responsible for systems analysis, programming, or equipment operation and maintenance also responsible for the security of the systems because there isn't sufficient separation of duties. Also, the computer specialist reports to an individual who is responsible for these activities, which is an internal control weakness since the specialist would need to be able to override the manager's decisions.

➢ **Develop systems and applications security plans.** The FWS reported that 5 of the 9 general support systems and 2 of the 3 major applications did not have security policies and procedures, risk assessments, and contingency plans. These policies, procedures, practices, and plans are the basis for security plans; therefore, we believe that it is unlikely that security plans existed.

The FWS management did not hold information resources personnel or other personnel, such as system owners, accountable for ensuring Federal minimum security controls were in place and operating effectively for the FWS' general support systems and major applications.

Additionally, although the FWS identified material weaknesses in the areas of risk assessments and contingency planning for its general support systems and major applications, the FWS did not report to the Department's Chief Information Officer that it had an overall information systems security control weakness. The FWS did not report this weakness because the FWS had developed

15

action plans to correct the weaknesses; however, the plans were not scheduled for completion until after fiscal year 2000. Until the corrective actions have been implemented, we will continue to report the control weaknesses over the FWS' general support systems and major applications as a reportable condition. Additionally, we will report these weaknesses as a reportable condition in our report on compliance with laws and regulations related to our audit of the FWS' fiscal year 2000 financial statements.

Recommendations

We recommend that the FWS:

    1. Assign appropriate individuals security responsibility at each of its installations.

    2. Develop security plans for each general support system and major application.

    3. Hold information resources personnel and other personnel accountable for developing and implementing adequate security over the FWS' general support systems and major applications.

The FWS Response: The FWS agrees with this finding and recommendations. The FWS will:

- Prepare a compilation of each FWS installation together with a documented assignment of security responsibility for each site; list the site and the person assigned responsibility, accompanied by a formal assignment of security responsibility to that individual based on an analysis of the appropriate nature of assigning such responsibility to the individual. The FWS will secure Departmental waivers where needed.
- Identify all general support systems and major applications; identify which systems and applications do not have security plans; work with the managers of the systems and applications to review security controls and training and correct weaknesses; and work with the managers to develop or update security plans.
- Develop a multi-year Management Control Review cycle for general support systems and major applications in accordance with 270 FW 4, "IRM Reviews".

16

Stewardship and Performance Measures

We considered the FWS' internal controls over the Required Supplementary Stewardship Information by obtaining an understanding of the FWS' internal controls, determining whether these internal controls had been placed in operation, assessing control risks, and performing tests of controls as required by OMB Bulletin 01-02. Our review was not of sufficient scope to provide assurance on these controls. Accordingly, we do not provide an opinion on such controls. We have, however, applied certain limited procedures, which consisted principally of inquiries of management regarding the methods of measurement and presentation of the Required Supplementary Stewardship Information. In applying these limited procedures, we believe that the FWS' lack of reporting Stewardship investments made by grantees in non-Federal physical property represents a material departure from the reporting requirements in the Statement of Federal Financial Accounting Standards Number 8, Supplementary Stewardship Reporting.

With respect to internal controls related to performance measures reported in the FWS' Annual Report, we obtained an understanding of the design of the significant internal controls relating to the existence and completeness assertions, as required by OMB Bulletin 01-02. Our procedures were not designed to provide assurance over internal controls over reported performance measures, and accordingly, we do not provide an opinion on such controls

G. Stewardship Investments

The FWS has not reported on stewardship investments in non-Federal physical property made by grantees in fiscal year 2000, as required by the Statement of Federal Financial Accounting Standards Number 8, Supplementary Stewardship Reporting. In fiscal year 1999, however, the FWS reported on stewardship investments of $191.2 million that were made by grantees for acquiring and improving non-Federal physical property. The FWS' lack of reporting stewardship investments made by grantees in non-Federal physical property in fiscal year 2000 represents a departure from the reporting requirements.

Recommendation

We recommend that the FWS report on stewardship investments funded through grants for non-Federal physical property.

17

The FWS Response: The FWS disagrees with this finding. The FWS maintains that the intent for reporting stewardship investments is to identify funds that are directed toward or result in maintaining or enhancing the national productive capacity. Using this definition the FWS believes that its grant programs, which include investments, to acquire and improve non-Federal physical property do not qualify as stewardship investments.

The OIG Reply: The FWS asserts that the intent for reporting stewardship investments is to identify funds that maintain or enhance national productive capacity. However, the definitions of "stewardship investments" and "non-Federal physical property" contained in the Statement of Federal Financial Accounting Standards Number 8, Supplementary Stewardship Reporting do not support FWS' position. We therefore consider this recommendation unresolved.

Report on Compliance With Laws and Regulations

Management of the FWS is responsible for complying with applicable laws and regulations. As part of obtaining reasonable assurance as to whether the FWS' financial statements are free of material misstatement, we performed tests of the FWS' compliance with certain provisions of laws and regulations, noncompliance with which could have a direct and material effect on the determination of financial statement amounts, and certain other laws and regulations specified in OMB Bulletin 01-02, including the requirements referred to in the Federal Financial Management Improvement Act (FFMIA) of 1996. We limited our tests of compliance to these provisions, and we did not test compliance with all laws and regulations applicable to the FWS.

As discussed in the internal control finding C, the FWS is not in compliance with the Code of Federal Regulations (43 CFR), Uniform Administrative Requirements for Grants and Cooperative Agreements to State and Local Governments, Part 12.81(b), which stipulates that grantees will report on the status of funds using the SF-269, Financial Status Report--Long Form, or SF-269A, Financial Status Report--Short Form. This matter is discussed as a material weakness with recommendations in our report on internal controls.

Under the FFMIA, we are required to report whether the FWS financial management systems substantially comply with: (1)

18

Federal financial management system requirements, (2) applicable Federal accounting standards, and (3) the U.S. Government Standard General Ledger at the transaction level. To meet our reporting requirements, we performed tests of compliance with the FFMIA section 803(a) requirements. The results of our tests disclosed instances described below where the FWS' financial management system did not substantially comply with applicable Federal accounting standards and Federal financial system requirements.

> The FWS was not complying with Federal accounting standards regarding stewardship investments for fiscal year 2000. The Statement of Federal Financial Accounting Standards Number 8, Supplementary Stewardship Reporting, establishes standards for reporting on the Federal Government's stewardship over certain resources and responsibilities, including stewardship investments. The standard identifies stewardship investments as "Non-Federal Physical Property–grants provided for properties financed by the Federal Government, but owned by the state and local governments." This matter is discussed as a finding with recommendations in the preceding Stewardship and Performance Measures section of this report.

> The FWS was not in full compliance with Federal financial system requirements. Office of Management and Budget Circular A-130, "Management of Federal Information Resources," Appendix III, "Security of Federal Automated Information Resources," requires that adequate security be provided for all agency information collected, processed, transmitted, stored, or disseminated in general support systems and major applications. We noted certain matters, which indicate that the FWS was not complying with Office of Management and Budget Circular A-130, Appendix III, "Security of Federal Automated Information Resources." These matters are discussed as a reportable condition with recommendations in our report on internal controls.

The results of our tests disclosed no instances in which the FWS' financial management system did not substantially comply with the United States General Ledger at the transaction level.

Providing an opinion on compliance with certain provisions of laws and regulations was not an objective of our audit and, accordingly, we do express such an opinion.

19

PRIOR AUDIT COVERAGE

We reviewed prior Office of Inspector General and General Accounting Office audit reports related to the FWS' financial statements to determine whether these reports contained any unresolved or unimplemented recommendations that were significant to the FWS financial statements or internal controls. The results of this review are in Appendix 2.

We made 19 recommendations addressing the weaknesses that we identified. Based on the FWS' May 18, 2001 response (Appendix 3) to the draft audit report, we consider 2 recommendations unresolved and 17 recommendations resolved but not implemented. Accordingly, the recommendations that are not resolved or implemented will be referred to the Assistant Secretary for Policy, Management and Budget for resolution and tracking of implementation.

Section 5(a) of the Inspector General Act (5 U.S.C. app. 3) requires the Office of Inspector General to list this report in its semiannual report to the Congress. In addition, the Office of Inspector General provides audit reports to the Congress.

This report is intended for the information of management of the Department of the Interior, the Office of Management and Budget, and the Congress. However, this report is a matter of public record, and its distribution is not limited.

Roger La Rouche
Assistant Inspector General
for Audits
February 14, 2001

Objective, Scope, and Methodology

Management of the FWS is responsible for the following:

> ➤ Preparing the principal financial statements and the required supplementary information in conformity with generally accepted accounting principles and for preparing the other information contained in the Annual Report for fiscal year 2000.

> ➤ Establishing and maintaining an internal control structure over financial reporting. In fulfilling this responsibility, estimates and judgments are required to assess the expected benefits and related costs of internal control structure policies and procedures.

> ➤ Complying with applicable laws and regulations.

We are responsible for the following:

> ➤ Expressing an opinion on the FWS' principal financial statements.

> ➤ Obtaining an understanding of the internal controls based on the internal control objectives contained in OMB Bulletin 01-02, which require that transactions be properly recorded, processed, and summarized to permit the preparation of the principal financial statements and the required supplementary information in accordance with Federal accounting standards; that assets be safeguarded against loss from unauthorized acquisition, use, or disposal; and that transactions and other data that support reported performance measures be properly recorded, processed, and summarized to permit the preparation of performance information in accordance with criteria stated by management.

> ➤ Testing the FWS' compliance with selected provisions of laws and regulations that could materially affect the principal financial statements or the required supplementary information.

To fulfill these responsibilities, we took the following actions:

> ➤ Examined, on a test basis, evidence supporting the amounts disclosed in the principal financial statements.

> ➤ Assessed the accounting principles used and the significant estimates made by management.

> ➤ Evaluated the overall presentation of the principal financial statements.

21

> Obtained an understanding of the internal control structure related to safeguarding assets; compliance with laws and regulations, including the execution of transactions in accordance with budget authority; financial reporting; and certain performance measure information reported in the annual report.

> Tested relevant internal controls over the safeguarding of assets; compliance with laws and regulations, including the execution of transactions in accordance with budget authority; and financial reporting.

> Tested compliance with selected provisions of laws and regulations.

We did not evaluate all of the internal controls related to the operating objectives as broadly defined by the Federal Managers' Financial Integrity Act, such as those controls related to preparing statistical reports and ensuring efficient operations. We limited our internal control testing to those controls needed to achieve the objectives outlined in our report on internal controls.

PRIOR AUDIT COVERAGE

We reviewed prior Office of Inspector General and General Accounting Office audit reports related to the FWS' financial statements to determine whether these reports contained any unresolved or unimplemented recommendations that were significant to the FWS' financial statements or internal controls. We found two reports issued by the Office of Inspector General that contained significant unimplemented recommendations related to the FWS' financial statements or internal controls:

> "Deferred Maintenance, U. S. Fish and Wildlife Service," Report No. 00-I-226, issued March 10, 2000. Funding for the FWS deferred maintenance projects was not spent solely on the FWS' highest priority deferred maintenance projects. Of the $93.2 million available in fiscal years 1996 through 1998 for deferred maintenance, $4.8 million was spent on non-maintenance expenses such as equipment replacements, administrative functions, and routine maintenance. In addition, the FWS needed to improve the reliability of its deferred maintenance data. The deferred maintenance data prepared for the FWS' fiscal year 1998 financial statements were not reliable because the FWS failed to survey all of its assets to determine its deferred maintenance needs, had not fully documented its estimated deferred maintenance costs, and had not established adequate controls over deferred maintenance data. To correct these deficiencies, the OIG recommended that the FWS ensure that deferred maintenance funds are allocated to field offices on the basis of priority and that the FWS implement controls over the expenditure of deferred maintenance funding and controls over deferred maintenance data. All recommendations are resolved, and three recommendations are implemented.

> "Miscellaneous Receipts, U. S. Fish and Wildlife Service," Report No. 00-I-50, issued November 9, 1999. This review of 46 refuges operated by the FWS revealed that 5 refuges charged unauthorized fees for the mitigation of damages associated with oil and gas exploration and then arranged for the fees to be retained for refuge use. At the 46 FWS refuges visited or contacted, the FWS set fees for the use of refuge resources that provided a reasonable return to the Government. However, five refuges in Louisiana and Texas assessed fees of more than $32.8 million during fiscal years 1990-1998, depositing only $26 million into U.S. Treasury accounts, as required by law. At the five refuges, the FWS directed exploration companies to deposit fees of $1.5 million into accounts maintained by the Fish and Wildlife Foundation, to remit fees of $5.1 million into the refuges' contributed funds accounts, and to pay fees of about $200,000 to vendors and grantees. The refuges used the fees for expenses such as employee salaries, marine-related equipment and repairs, computers, research grants, travel, fuel, a vehicle, and lumber. In addition, the OIG questioned the FWS' retention of about $21.3 million from fiscal years 1990 through 1998 for the costs of administering economic uses on the refuges because the FWS had not determined the amount of its administrative expenses in accordance with the Provisions of the Refuge Revenue Sharing Act. The Office of the Solicitor, the OIG, and the FWS reached resolution in August 2000. The FWS is taking action to implement the recommendations.

23

United States Department of the Interior

FISH AND WILDLIFE SERVICE
Washington, D.C. 20240

IN REPLY REFER TO:

FWS/DF

MAY 1 8 2001

Memorandum

To: Regional Audit Manager - Central Region
          Acting Office of Inspector General

From: Director   *[signature]*

Subject: Draft Independent Auditors Report on the U.S. Fish and Wildlife Service's Financial
          Statements for FY 2000

The opportunity to review and comment on the subject draft report is sincerely appreciated. In this review, the Service reiterates its general agreement with the report. Suggestions for revising the paraphrased Service responses are provided, as well as more detailed information on actions taken or planned to implement OIG recommendations. The Service disagrees with the findings on compliance with laws and regulations and the bases for our conclusions are set forth. The Service also requests revisions be made to the report on prior audit coverage in order to improve the accuracy of Appendix 2.

Report on Internal Controls

The Service generally agrees with the draft report on internal controls and with the presentation of the Service's response to these findings. The Service would like to see the final report continue to use the same format as the draft, whereby the sections entitled, "FWS Response," are retained. However, the Service highlights below a few specific changes to the text of select responses to clarify the paraphrased response of the Service.

It should also be noted that both the OIG and the Service reached a jointly held understanding regarding the reporting of certain findings as material internal control weaknesses. As explicitly mentioned in the draft report, recommendations for reporting specified findings to the Department of the Interior as material internal control weaknesses will remain open to further consideration until September 30, 2001. The need to carefully consider which weaknesses to report as material control weaknesses in response to the Federal Managers' Financial Integrity Act (FMFIA) requirements, arises due to the different definitions of material weaknesses used in both the FMFIA and the financial statement audit processes and the different time periods for each process. The status of the corrective actions taken by the Service will be reviewed at the end of FY 2001 to determine whether the findings should be reported as material weaknesses under the FMFIA.

24

Undelivered Orders

The Service agrees with the finding and with the recommendations. To clarify the Service's response, the following revisions to the text are suggested:

- OIG Finding - First bullet: the last sentence should be revised to read: "(Subsequently, the FWS Finance Center researched the reconciling items in the Region's report and found there were substantially fewer reconciling items totaling less than $3 million.)"

- FWS Response - The second paragraph should be revised to acknowledge that the Service has: (1) continued its comprehensive review of UDO discrepancies between the Federal Aid Information Management System (FAIMS) and the Service's financial system (FFS); (2) improved the monthly FAIMS/FFS reconciliation process; and (3) implemented a quarterly review process for UDO's that remain unchanged for a year.

To timely address remaining Federal Aid differences, the Service has taken the following actions:

- Staff from the Federal Aid headquarters and Regional offices conducted a workshop in March 2001 to reconcile remaining differences between FFS and FAIMS. During the workshop, nearly 200 differences between the systems were identified, all of which are differences that predate the revised interface and reconciliation processes implemented in FY 2000. Of the total, 90 percent of the discrepancies were reconciled at the workshop and the remaining 10 percent are currently being researched.
  Target Date: June 30, 2001.

- Improved policies and procedures for timely reconciling and correcting monthly discrepancies between FAIMS and FFS were drafted at the workshop. The document identifies actions required to improved oversight of monthly reconciliations of the two systems, establishes monthly time lines for reconciliation, and assigns responsibility to appropriate officials.
  Target Date: June 30, 2001.

Construction-in-Progress

The Service agrees with the finding and with the recommendations. Below are detailed actions being taken by the task force established specifically for addressing this finding:

- Develop improved reconciliation procedures - The Service is currently developing strengthened guidance for reconciling the Construction Work-in-Progress (WIP) account to internal property records. The guidance provides timeframes, definitions, duties and responsibilities.
  Target Date: May 18, 2001

- Implement procedures for recording capital projects in the WIP account - The Service is investigating system changes to minimize recording expense transactions in the WIP account. Target Date: June 30, 2001

Processes Used by Grantees to Document and Support Costs Incurred For Federal Aid Program Grants

The Service agrees with the finding and with the recommendations. Below are detailed actions taken or being planned to implement the recommendations:

- The Chief, Division of Federal Aid will prepare a policy for the Director's signature requiring recipients of Federal Aid multi-year grants to submit annual financial status reports (SF-269's) at the end of each grant year. (Recipients of single-year grants are already required to submit SF-269's within 90 days of the end of the grant year.) Target Date: July 1, 2001.

- The Chief Division of Federal Aid, in consultation with the Division of Finance, will develop an accrual process for unbilled grant expenses based on an analysis of recipient spending patterns for various types of grants for use in accruing grant expenses at FY 2001 yearend. Target Date: September 1, 2001.

Capitalized Equipment Reconciliation Procedures and Procedures for Recording Capitalized Equipment Transactions

The Service recognizes the need to improve the accuracy of the initial recording of capitalized equipment transactions and the procedures used to reconcile and correct errors in FFS and Service property systems. To establish revised Service policies and procedures, the Assistant Director-Business Management and Operations will establish a workgroup consisting of representatives from the Divisions of Contracting and General Services and Finance and Regional Property Officials to evaluate current processes and property systems. The workgroup will develop specific procedural guidance to be followed in identifying and correcting the causes of errors. The workgroup will evaluate existing property systems to determine if existing systems meet legal and functional requirements. If it is determined that existing systems cannot readily be modified to include additional common data elements and improved edits, the Service will consult with Departmental officials on the availability of replacement systems.
Target Date: December 30, 2001

Pending the completion of the workgroup's effort, the Service will:

- provide specific guidance to all Regional Offices on the importance of the correct use of budget object classes (BOC); and
- direct that training be conducted by Regional Offices for both administrative and property officers and that this training emphasize the correct use of BOCs. Target Date: July 31, 2001.

Improved General Controls Over Automated Systems

The Service agrees with these findings and with the recommendations. Below is the Service's action plan to implement the three recommendations. These actions will be taken under the leadership of the Division of Information Resources Management on behalf of the Service.

- Assign appropriate individuals security responsibility at each of its installations - The Service will: prepare a compilation of each Service installation together with a documented assignment of security responsibility for each site; list the site and the person assigned responsibility, accompanied by a formal assignment of security responsibility to that individual based on an analysis of the appropriate nature of assigning such responsibility to the individual. The Service will secure Departmental waivers where needed.
  Target Date: November 30, 2001

- Develop security plans for each general support system and major application - The Service will: identify all general support systems (GSS) and major applications; identify which GSS and major applications do not have security plans; work with owners and managers of GSS and major systems to review their security controls and training, and to correct weaknesses; and, work with system owners and managers to develop or update security plans.
  Target Date: February 22, 2002

- Hold information resources personnel and other personnel accountable for developing and implementing adequate security over FWS' general support systems and major applications - The Service will develop a multi-year Management Control Review (MCR) review cycle for GSS and major applications in accordance with 270 FW 4, "IRM Reviews".
  Target Date: November 30, 2001

Report on Compliance with Laws and Regulations

Accounting Standards Governing Stewardship Investments

The intent of the Statement of Federal Financial Accounting Standards 8 (SSFAS #8) for reporting Stewardship Investments is to identify funds provided by Federal agencies to grant recipients that are directed toward or result in maintaining or enhancing the national productive capacity. The Service's interpretation of this standard is that it does not report under this standard as none of the three target investment areas mentioned in SSFAS #8 – land purchases, research and development (R&D), and human capital (training) – apply to Service grant programs. The OIG agrees with the Service that SSFAS #8 does not apply to Service grants regarding two of the three target investments, that is R&D and training. The Service continues to believe that there is no basis to conclude that purchases of lands made with funds provided in part by Service grants for the expressed purposes of conservation contributes to maintaining or enhancing national economic productivity.

OMB Circular A-130 Governing Security for Automated Information Systems

The Service acknowledges that the recommended improvements to general controls are needed as discussed in the report on internal controls; however, the Service believes that it has otherwise substantially implemented the requirements of Transmittal 3 of OMB Circular A-130, which was applicable to FY 2000 operations. For your consideration, the Service has: assigned responsibility for security; issued Servicewide guidelines governing the acceptable use of Service IT systems; initiated risk assessment procedures to identify acceptable levels of risk for Service systems; provided security training opportunities for all employees; developed a basic incident response capability for security issues; instituted continuity of operations plans and contingency plans for Y2K initiatives; and, certified and accredited general support systems and major applications consistent with DOI guidelines.

Prior Audit Coverage

Appendix 2 describes the status of three prior audits. To improve the accuracy of Appendix 2, the Service requests the OIG consider the following updated information and changes for the three audit reports mentioned:

- Deferred Maintenance, FWS, Report No. 00-I-226 - In the response to the final report, the Service clarified its intended implementing action for the recommendation the OIG considered unresolved. In the OIG's May 18, 2000, memorandum to the Assistant Secretary for Policy, Management and Budget, the OIG considered all recommendations resolved and three recommendations implemented. Therefore, please delete the last three sentences and replace them with: "All recommendations are resolved, and three recommendations are implemented."

- Miscellaneous Receipts, FWS, Report No. 00-1-50 - Please add the following sentences: "The Office of the Solicitor, OIG, and FWS reached resolution in August 2000. FWS is taking action to implement the recommendations."

- Financial Management Review of the U.S. Fish and Wildlife Service's Reported Allocation of Resources for its Refuge Program and New Assistant Regional Manager Positions, Report No. GAO/AIMD-00-84R - The Service disagrees that there are any unresolved or unimplemented recommendations from this audit. The Department's response to the U.S. General Accounting Office's (GAO) final presentation and briefing materials described our implementation of GAO's recommendation. The information we have regarding the Office of Financial Management's (PFM) tracking list indicates that PFM is not tracking any open recommendations from this audit. Please delete all references to this GAO audit report in your report.

The Service appreciates your considerations concerning our comments. If you have any questions or need more information, please contact the Assistant Director - Business Management and Operations directly by calling (202) 208- 4888.

STATUS OF AUDIT RECOMMENDATIONS

Finding/ Recommendation Reference	Status	Action Required
B.2 and G	Unresolved.	No further response to the Office of Inspector General is required. The recommendations will be referred to the Assistant Secretary for Policy, Management and Budget for resolution.
A.1, A.2, A.3, A.4, B. 1, B.3, C.1, C.2, C.3, D.1, D.2, D.3, E.1, E.2, F.1, F.2, and F.3	Resolved; not implemented.	No further response to the Office of Inspector General is required. The recommendations will be forwarded to the Assistant Secretary for Policy, Management and Budget for tracking of implementation. The target dates and titles of the officials responsible for implementation should be provided to the Office of Financial Management.

29

Supplemental Information
Performance Costs under the Service's Program Goals

Under the Results Act and as presented in total in Service budget documents, the Service established three mission goals under which to measure its performance. This chart represents Service performance costs under each mission goal for FY 2000.

	Consolidating Information			
	Habitat Sustainability of Fish and Wildlife Populations	*Conservation: A Network of Lands and Water*	*Public Use and Enjoyment*	*Consolidated Total*
PROGRAM EXPENSES:				
Operating Expenses				
With Federal Agencies	$80,454	$87,275	$37,779	$ 205,508
With the Public	480,427	801,151	127,979	1,409,557
Total Operating Expenses	560,881	888,426	165,758	1,615,065
Interest Expense				
With the Public	14	45	5	64
Total Interest Expense	14	45	5	64
Depreciation and Amortization	15,669	16,874	7,634	40,177
Bad Debt Expense	(30)	4	4	(22)
Expenses Not Requiring Budgetary Resources	6,309	6,794	3,074	16,177
Other Gains and Losses	456	491	222	1,169
Total Program Expenses	583,299	912,634	176,697	1,672,630
PROGRAM REVENUES:				
Sale of Goods and Services to Federal Agencies	(26,584)	(37,934)	(8,331)	(72,849)
Sale of Goods and Services to the Public	(5,876)	(4,970)	(561)	(11,407)
Total Sale of Goods and Services	(32,460)	(42,904)	(8,892)	(84,256)
Other Revenues	(8,198)	(39,422)	(2,887)	(50,507)
Total Program Revenues	(40,658)	(82,326)	(11,779)	(134,763)
NET COST OF OPERATIONS	$542,641	$830,308	$164,918	$1,537,867

U.S. Department of the Interior
U.S. Fish & Wildlife Service
http://www.fws.gov

April 2001